MW01156302

The Three of Us

A memoir by:
Summerlin Conner

For Andrew and Lucy, my two most favorite people

Table of Contents:

Chapter 1: *The Beginning*

I became a single parent in October 2012. No big deal, right? I'm pretty sure millions of people all over the world do it every year. Wikipedia says there are around twelve million single parents in the United States alone. Perfect. This meant I was definitely not alone.

When I got divorced, I envisioned long days of quality time with my kids, watching whatever I wanted on TV, having a whole king-sized bed to myself, lots of quiet time to work on myself and rebuild my life after divorce, vacation adventures with just me and the kids, and a fresh start to life! I envisioned working through my post-divorce emotions in a healthy, proactive way and spending time with supportive friends and family. I envisioned building a new life that was filled with hope, joy, happiness, and good times!

Fast forward seven or so years later. Instead, I have been through sleepless nights, multiple dating disasters, and countless kid meltdowns. I have been on the brink of foreclosure and bankruptcy, dealing with lawyers, and I have had to move three times. I have had to tackle kid troubles in school, bad grades, meeting with counselors, and never-ending class projects. On top of financial nightmares, I have had car breakdowns and even my own breakdowns as I struggled with loneliness and relentless fatigue. On top of all of that, I somehow managed to gain thirty pounds (yes thirty!) which only added to my misery. I have had moments of sheer joy, moments of absolute desperation, and literally everything in between.

I can't even tell you the number of times I have cried in my bathroom because of the weight of responsibility I have felt due to being a single parent. I can't tell you the number of times I have sat in my bed and prayed to God to please get me through this. I can't tell you the number of times I did not think I would survive.

But I also can't tell you how many times I have beamed with pride when I looked at my kids. I can't tell you the number of times I have secretly cried with joy when my kids woke me up with homemade Mother's Day gifts. I can't tell you how many times a hug from my son or daughter reminded me why I need to keep going or the number of times I have thought to myself that I would not trade even one minute of this mess for anything different.

If you have ever been divorced and you have children, you already know what a hot mess this whole situation can be. From the day you and your ex split up to every day after that it can be easy to mistake your life for a roller coaster ride at times. Seriously. Like there should be safety harnesses for this ride. Getting divorced is messy enough by itself and then you add kids to the mix. Sheesh.

The whole process of getting divorced and becoming a single parent is an oftentimes downright unpleasant adventure. So many decisions to make. Who will live where? Who will go where and when? Who will pick up who from school? Who will pay for this? Who will pay for that? And on and on and on. And the catch is that all of these decisions typically need to be made during a time in which emotions are already running pretty high. Everyone is working on molding themselves into a new role and things can get really sticky. And on top of all that, it's quite possible that one or both of the parents will be moving in and/or out of old or new houses, which adds its own long to-do list to the mix.

Oh, I am absolutely certain that there are single parents out there who moved through this whole process with grace and ease as if it were just a little blip on the radar that needed some minor adjustments. And, yes, I can absolutely think of a trillion worse things that could happen besides getting divorced and becoming a single parent. When I really think about it, divorce and single parenting are not the end of the world in the grand scheme of things. Definitely not.

But that does not mean it's easy. And I will be the very first to admit that I do not belong to the aforementioned group of people who have moved through this process with grace and ease. I am more like a bull in a china shop. More like a kidney stone. More like fingernails on a chalkboard. But I didn't come to realize this right away. At first, I honestly believed I would belong to the grace and ease group. I thought I could handle whatever came up without missing a beat. I assumed that I would be the poster child for divorcing moms who are winning this game!

Well, not so fast. Divorce was hard—really, really hard. And becoming a single mom may have been even harder. There were so many times when I did not think I could go on a minute longer. And so many times I felt so freaking lonely. And so many unexpected twists and turns. And the whole process left me feeling like I was so different from all the other parents who were still married. I felt isolated and like I did not fit in. I didn't know anyone else who was in the same position. I didn't have any friends who were going through the same thing. At the time, I was the only single mom in my group of friends.

Over the years, I have put in countless hours listening to motivational podcasts, reading self-help books, and doing all the things we're advised to do. I have tried meditating, yoga, reiki, etc. You name it, I have probably done it. All of these things are fabulous and really are super helpful, but what I realized is none of these things really related to what I was going through, or at least it didn't feel like it.

A lot of the self-help books would suggest things like, "Ask your husband to watch the kids a few mornings during the week so you can have some you time!" Um, okay. That sounds great and all but I don't have a husband. Or I would listen to a podcast and be told, "Hey single moms! Set aside just $150 a month and you can be rich!" Oh jeez. When you aren't even sure if you have enough money for gas to get to work, $150 isn't really easy to set aside.

And, to be really honest, there is only so much deep breathing you can do when it comes to facing foreclosure and there are only so many downward dog poses you can do to feel better when your car just broke down for the second time. Anyway, I kept on keeping on and I read the books and I listened to the podcasts and they definitely helped, but I continued to feel somewhat isolated.

Somewhere along the way, during my lowest point, I started to write about all of it. I wrote everything down. And as it poured out of me I started to feel better. Maybe it was because I was getting it all out. I don't know. But I started feeling better and, to be honest, I started laughing about it. I mean like laugh out loud laughing. Laughing until my belly hurt. I know; sounds like I am obviously completely nuts. But really, I wrote as though I were talking to a close friend who understood exactly what I was going through and we were having a good laugh over it. I wrote as though I were in a single parent support group filled with like-minded people who were going through the trenches right alongside me. As if I were talking to them. As though we were looking at each other and saying, "I know, right?" And I felt understood! I felt better. And when I put down all of my misfortunes, awkward feelings, and nightmarish despair on paper, I felt stronger. I felt proud of myself for surviving the, in my opinion, shitstorm known as divorce and becoming a single parent. And when I sat back and really looked at it from an outsider's perspective, all I could do was laugh.

So I kept writing. And I kept feeling better. And I am pretty sure I wrote my way out of my funk. And then it occurred to me that if I was feeling so isolated and different going through this process, maybe there were other people feeling the same way. I decided to start writing about things that seemingly only another single parent would really understand.

So, although I undoubtedly run the risk of major embarrassment by sending my story out into the world, I am hoping that some single parent who is out there and feeling super crappy right about now can relate. Maybe some lonely mom or dad can have a good laugh at my expense and feel better for just a minute. Maybe someone who feels like they are in a situation that feels unsurvivable will feel motivated to keep going. Maybe the stories I share can resonate with someone who feels isolated. I really hope so.

Chapter 2: *Crickets*

I don't remember the very first time my kids went to spend time with their dad and I was left home alone. I don't know if it was for a night, a weekend, or just dinner. I don't remember what day of the week it was. What I vividly remember is the immediate deafening silence of the house when they left. I remember feeling disoriented and anxious without having them home with me. I remember the hours creeping by as I awaited their return.

When my ex-husband and I divorced, we shared custody of the kids with him having the kids every other weekend and Wednesday nights. I had them the rest of the time. My kids were around 8 and 10 years old at the time. Initially, I started looking forward to a little break and time alone every other weekend and Wednesday nights. I would start making a list of all the things I would get done when the kids were away. I would daydream about long, uninterrupted bubble baths, long walks, and going to the grocery store all alone. I daydreamed about watching whatever I wanted on TV and spending long afternoons reading good books. I imagined all of the things I would get done and how peaceful it would be.

And then the kids would leave. As soon as they walked out the door for Dad's house, I would be just wonderful for about five minutes. I would quickly get to work on all the exciting things I had been looking forward to. I would make a nice cup of warm tea, get my favorite jammies on, and break out that new book I couldn't wait to start reading. Or I would put my workout clothes on and head out the door for a much needed walk. Or I would sit down at my desk to go over bills and paperwork while I had some quiet time. Or, better yet, bake some cookies and watch that movie I had been dying to see.

And then, sitting alone in my house, all I could hear were crickets. No footsteps, no kids' TV shows, no screaming, no fighting, no crying, no trampoline springs squealing, nobody yelling for me to bring them a glass of water, no nothing. Just crickets.

This was the point in time when I would start feeling anxiety creeping in, disorientation creeping in. I felt really uncomfortable. Really miserable. I missed them so much. It was like a part of me was literally missing. I didn't know what to do without them. I spent a lot of time crying and wishing I could get them back home. Those first weekends, or probably the first year of weekends to be honest, were no fun. Okay, honestly, they were sheer misery. Like torture. I would anxiously plow through the weekend trying to jam as much work or projects or whatever into it as I could. I tried to hurry time up. It's so strange because I would start wondering what on earth I had been thinking when I was daydreaming about them being gone. I started thinking I would give anything for them to come home.

I started turning the volume up on the TV. I started putting on music to clean the house. I started running a totally unnecessary amount of errands so that I didn't have to sit at home. I started taking long walks. Like really long walks. Like, no joke, three-hour walks. Who even does that? Apparently me. I wanted to be gone from my house for as long as I could.

And when I did stop for a minute to think, I would start thinking about what the kids might be doing with Dad. Were they having fun? Were they enjoying their time with him more than the time they spent with me? Were they eating cotton candy and riding unicorns and buying toys? Were they telling Dad all about what a bad mom I was and how much they hated being with me? I know, this is kind of over-the-top thinking, but, honestly, that's exactly how my thinking would go. I would mull this stuff over for the longest time and convince myself that at any minute I would hear from the kids saying that they had decided that they liked Dad better and they would be living with him full time now. Or, even worse, I envisioned them coming home to pack their suitcases and wish me a final goodbye before moving to Dad's permanently. And they would probably say something like, "Look Mom, we love you and all, but Dad's house is nicer and he has better Wi-Fi." I mean could you blame them?

One of the many aspects of divorce that you may not necessarily see coming is the crushing loneliness that can come on. For some reason, when the house is empty, it's like the silence is magnified and you just become so aware of being alone. Just having other warm bodies in the house, even if you are in totally separate rooms and not speaking to each other, provides a bit of relief from feeling so alone. At times, when I have been alone in my house, I have seriously sat and pondered over what I would do if there were an intruder, or a fire, or the house collapsed and it was just me all alone. What if I screamed for help and nobody heard me? What if I were trapped under a pile of rubble and left for the buzzards? Anyway, in my opinion, there should be more than one person in the house.

So, Sunday evenings would inevitably roll around and I would start to get excited. The kids would be coming home the next day! I would spend Sunday evenings going to the grocery store and getting their favorite foods. I would bake cookies to have ready for them when they came home. And I would plan out my whole Monday so that I could be sure to finish work early and be first in the carpool line to pick them up from school. My plan would be to be ready and waiting upon their arrival with Chick-fil-A kids' meals and lots of hugs and kisses. I was positive that their arrival back home would bring much needed joy and excitement back to my house. Gone would be the dreadful quiet and excruciating loneliness. We would all sit on the couch and talk about our weekends and how much we missed each other. Maybe we would play some board games and maybe even go out for ice cream! I couldn't wait! I would go to sleep on Sunday nights filled with anticipation knowing that my time in this torturous isolation was almost over.

And then Monday would arrive and they would come home. I am not kidding when I say that it would take about six minutes and I would be wishing that they would go back to their dad's. As soon as they got home, they would be whining about something, fighting with each other, telling me there was no food in the house, demanding that I take them to the Mexican restaurant, and, in general, being little jerks. What happened to snuggling on the couch and telling stories about our weekends? What happened to lots of hugs and kisses and going for ice cream? I would practically be kicking myself for not realizing the value and beauty of my alone time that I had just taken for granted. What had I been thinking? Can we have a do over? Can we start the weekend again and I swear I will cherish every minute? Please? And the really sad thing is that this went on for years. Literally years. I would miss them terribly when they left, be desperate for them to come back, and then immediately want to kill them when they did come home.

When I got divorced, my children became my whole world. They became my everything and when they were away I would feel horrible. I felt like a part of me was missing. I don't know if this is just a single parent thing or not. I know most parents miss their kids when they leave, but I would describe myself missing my kids as slightly psychotic. I have often sat and daydreamed about the fact that this is literally something that non-divorced parents will never really experience. I see pictures of intact families posting their weekend adventures on Facebook and think to myself, *You will literally never know what it feels like to have your heart broken every other weekend when your kids say goodbye, and you will not ever know the despair that is felt when your child reaches a milestone while they are at the other parent's house for the weekend.*

I wouldn't know what else to call it besides sheer hell if, for instance, your son loses his first tooth and gets a visit from the tooth fairy all while staying at Dad's for the weekend. Or what if your daughter is over at her mom's house and rides her bike without training wheels for the very first time? Ugh. Seriously that is a whole different kind of torture right there. Every year when the holidays start rolling around or birthdays start approaching, I start to get a sinking feeling in the pit of my stomach. How will this go? Will we be able to work together and come up with a suitable plan to split up times with the kids so that it's fair? Will I spend all of Christmas Day crying on the floor and missing my kids because they are not with me? Will I miss my daughter blowing out her birthday candles? Will I not be the one who gets to set out their Easter baskets and put their favorite candies in them? Oh, the horror. Thankfully, and I mean really thankfully, everything has worked out so far. I am beyond thankful that I haven't missed a single Christmas morning with my kids since getting divorced. I don't even want to imagine that scenario. But, although I haven't missed a single Christmas morning, I have missed my kids on Christmas afternoons when they go to their dad's house. And that takes some serious getting used to.

My advice for spending holidays without your kids? Avoid it if at all possible. Really. And if you can't avoid it, go hang out with other family or friends. Or go to a movie. Or go serve a warm dinner to the homeless. Or get a job where help is needed on holidays. I mean unless you really want to sit at home and listen to the crickets on Christmas. No thanks.

I should point out, though, that this horrible loneliness does fade over time. At least it did for me. Thank the good heavens! I now really and truly look forward to my weekends alone and I don't even notice the silence anymore. I can relax, get things done, do things with friends, and I don't feel miserable like I used to. Don't get me wrong, I still miss my kids when they are gone but not in the same way that I used to.

So, considering that I have many, many hours of cricket time under my belt, I have definitely learned a few things from this:

1. It doesn't matter how loud I turn the TV up, the silence will still be there when I am missing my kids. So I may as well embrace it! I may as well make friends with the crickets instead of constantly trying to run from them. Honestly, I feel like this is just a ritual that newly single parents have to go through. Because I really don't think that there is anything that would have made me feel better when I was sitting there in silence. Nothing besides my kids coming home. But, as hard as it is to believe, the misery of the silence does pass. Eventually, I started loving my free time and taking full advantage of being alone!

2. Putting pressure on myself to get a trillion things done when the kids are gone is not the best idea. For quite a while, after my

divorce and when my kids started going to their dad's house on weekends, I would put all kinds of pressure on myself to get EVERYTHING done so that I could "relax" when the kids came home. Okay, so that's a bad idea. My weekend to-do list would be a mile long and I would wind up stressed out and exhausted. Finally, I had a revelation that maybe I should spend at least a little of my free time having fun and relaxing. Maybe I should do things I actually like and recharge my batteries. Maybe I shouldn't completely drain myself before Monday morning rolled around. Besides, jamming my weekend with work and chores didn't make me feel better or miss the kids any less. It actually made me feel worse, which in turn made me miss my kids more. But, much to my surprise, taking care of myself and doing things I actually like did make me feel better. I still missed the kids terribly, but I started feeling better.

3. Re-entry is a bitch. What in the heck am I talking about? Okay, hear me out. Every, or almost every, time my kids would come

back from spending time at their dad's house, the first twenty-four hours were rough. Like I said earlier, they would be fighting or demanding or being sassy. No matter how calm and peaceful and loving I was, they were wound up and hostile. Eventually I realized that maybe it was the transition, in and of itself, from house to house that was stressful on their little bodies and they were just acting out their feelings. And this broke my heart. Even though they never said so, maybe they internally felt the tension of transitioning between the two environments. Two different houses. Two different ways of living. Two different sets of rules. Even as an adult I can imagine that this would be no easy task. So, after coming to this realization, I gave them a free pass to be the complete assholes they needed to be during every re-entry.

4. They will always come back to me. Even though I spent a humiliating amount of time pondering over the possibility of my kids abandoning me and riding off into the night with their dad, this never happened. They

always came home. And, yes, their dad probably did have better Wi-Fi and maybe the kids did ride unicorns at his house, but they always returned after their weekends with him. And I truly am happy that they love their dad so much and love spending time with him. I wouldn't want my kids to have it any other way. But boy there is nothing sweeter than when they come home.

If you happen to be a newly single parent and you are, in fact, sitting on your couch right now listening to crickets, I feel you. I really do. I can hear that godforsaken silence right along with you. Just keep going. It really does get better. And, in the meantime, turn the TV up.

Chapter 3: *Guilt*

As a single parent, it feels like there is a never-ending supply of good old guilt. Always something to feel guilty for. Always something to beat myself up about or lie awake at 3:00 a.m. rehashing. A never-ending list of reasons to feel like a horrible human.

Maybe some single parents don't feel this way. Maybe some single parents stand strong in their confidence, feel proud of every single choice they make, and have firm boundaries that do not allow for any opportunity for guilty feelings to seep in. Maybe some single parents move through their days effortlessly and with a consistently clear conscience.

That would not be me. Clearly, I have issues. I can be made to feel guilty at the drop of a hat. My daughter cries because I put an apple in her lunch instead of an orange? You would think I murdered an orphan. My son gets pissed because I made him clean his room? Totally valid reason for me to feel like I just ran over an elderly couple with my car.

I have a problem with feeling guilty. And I think it was made worse when I became a single parent. For one, just getting divorced and breaking up my children's family was reason enough for a mound of guilty feelings. Ripping their worlds apart made me feel like I was ripping their little hearts out. And ever since then it does not take much for me to feel guilty. I have consistently felt the weight of the responsibility of their feelings and I have consistently felt obligated to try to protect them from further damage. I totally realize that this is probably ridiculous and blown way out of proportion, but okay. It is what it is.

To me, being a single parent involves one scenario after another that creates guilty feelings. When I first got divorced, I don't think I even realized that I was feeling guilty at first. But after some time, I started to change my behavior to keep my kids from getting upset. I would make sure they got everything (or close to it) that they asked for on their birthday list. I would pack their lunch just like they wanted. I would be the first mom to volunteer for school functions. I would clean their room for them. I would spend money that I didn't have to take them places they wanted to go. I would bend over backwards to keep them smiling. You could say I was the queen of overcompensation.

Overcompensating became my modus operandi. I probably did more damage to my kids by catering to them than if I hadn't. I am sure one day they will be hitting me up for therapy money. And then they will be lying on a therapist's couch saying something like, "Well, the thing is, I am utterly helpless because my mom did literally everything for me." Yikes.

What really is ridiculous also is that every time I did something for my kids that I was sure was necessary to their survival, they didn't really even get that into it or act as if I had just saved their life. I would literally bend over backwards for them and their reaction would be, "Meh."

I remember this one time I was absolutely certain that my children would die a slow, painful death if we didn't take a Caribbean vacation. I know, right? Pathetic. Maybe it was actually me who would die a slow, painful death without a Caribbean vacation? I don't know, whatever. Anyway, my kids had just finished the school year and everyone (literally everyone) was getting ready to go to the beach. Of course, I wanted to go too. But really I kept thinking that my kids would have so much fun, be so fulfilled, and just let go of their worries if we took a vacation. I thought they would somehow be deprived if we didn't escape to an exotic locale like everyone else was getting ready to do. I thought they would be disappointed in me if I didn't overextend myself and plan a getaway. So, I pushed my wallet as far as it would go and booked us a cruise. I did not tell the kids. I started scheming and planning in my mind and coming up with ideas to announce the big news. I just knew that this was going to be the greatest news of their lives! I knew they would immediately announce that I had won the mom of the year award!

I waited a few days for the right moment and then, filled with giddiness and excitement, made the announcement to them that we would be leaving in a few days to go on a CRUISE! Well, to say they were not nearly as enthusiastic as I was hoping they would be would be an understatement. "Oh, I was hoping to go to Florida." Say what? What? Are you kidding me right now? The most irritating thing is that I could tell by their expressions that they were FAKING excitement. I wanted to stab their eyeballs out and then immediately request a refund. Okay, calm down. Maybe they just need a quick minute to warm up to the idea and then, when they realize that I said CRUISE, they will start to get hyped.

Over the next few days, they did start to get excited. We started packing and planning and they were getting into it. When the time came, we boarded the ship, sailed away, and had what I would consider to be a mildly good time.

We did have some fun, we did see new places, and we did spend quality time together. We visited islands and saw monkeys and ate lots of ice cream. But we also had moments of boredom. We also spent way more money than I wanted to. And the kids also did their usual amount of complaining even though we were in paradise.

What I learned from this vacation is that my kids probably would have survived and, honestly, maybe even enjoyed it more if we would have just driven a few hours away to Florida. I realized that I did not need to work so hard to try to ensure that they felt like everyone else. I realized that, even if they looked disappointed for a few minutes, in the end, they would get over it if I told them we would not be vacationing in Fiji like Johnny's family. I realized that biannual luxury vacations are not, much to my surprise, crucial to the survival of my children.

I can't talk about guilt here and not mention the guilt that arises when you have been seemingly outdone by your children's other parent. I have had plenty of experience with this one. In my particular situation, my income is far exceeded by my ex-husband's.

How do you even begin to properly explain this to your children? It is so hard to say, "Well, I know Daddy bought you that Xbox, but I can't afford to get you anything right now other than a happy meal from McDonald's." How do you hide the massive amount of pain you feel and keep a giant smile on your face when you just can't keep up with their other parent? For me personally, when I am just trying to make ends meet and my child comes home from Dad's house with a new bike and two hundred dollars cash and wants to show you because they are so excited, it feels like a strong punch in the gut. I don't know how many times I have spent a week alone over summer vacation literally working as much as legally possible to make some extra money while my kids were gone with their dad on what I would consider a dream vacation. Don't get me wrong, I am so happy for my kids that they are blessed enough to have these experiences. I am so happy at the opportunities they have sometimes been given. And I am so thankful that they have a dad who does these things for them. But it is a true story that being the parent with the much smaller salary can be hard on your ego. And when you are pretty close to being broke but want to try your hardest to provide these types of things for them, it's a recipe for disaster. I am DEFINITELY guilty of taking my kids on vacations that I really couldn't afford. I am definitely guilty of spending money on them that I didn't really have in an effort to keep up and give them everything. And, while I am being honest, I should mention that the cold hard truth is that I wanted to go on these vacations and buy these things just as much, if not more, than the kids. Ugh.

A while back, when I was in the depths of financial despair and facing possible foreclosure on my house and/or bankruptcy, my son came home from his dad's house driving his new "graduation present". A new truck that I am pretty sure cost more than anything I, at the age of 46, had ever owned. After my initial shock, I had to hold back tears. My son did not know anything about any financial strain I had been having. He would never have guessed that, after seeing him drive up the driveway in that new truck, I would feel like a failure, less than enough, and unable to compete. It may sound absolutely ridiculous that I felt this way, but I did. And don't get me wrong, I absolutely want my kids to have all the things if they are able too. And I sure do hope they understand the value of these things and don't take anything for granted. But it can be really hard to swallow when you are feeling so low. Anyway, in an effort to be a super supportive mom, and after the shock of seeing my son in his new truck passed, I put on my big girl panties and smiled and asked him to take me for a ride.

Besides trying to keep up with the Joneses, I also have found that I have tried to reduce my guilt levels in the past by being the perfect parent. Sheesh, so ridiculous. Several years ago, I basically quit having a social life because of the guilt I felt when leaving the kids with a babysitter. I also pretty much quit drinking anything alcoholic ever. But I think that also had to do with feeling responsible for them and being the only adult in the house, which meant that I should probably be sober. I also felt very uncomfortable going on dates (on the rare occasions that I went on dates) because I didn't want my kids to feel like they weren't number one to me. I also completely, for the most part, abandoned my workout schedule because I hated leaving the kids alone at home, for even an hour, to go out for a jog. I wound up changing jobs several times so that I could find the perfect job that would least interfere with my kids' schedule. I basically molded my entire life to be at their beck and call, which I don't think is necessarily the worst thing I could ever do. Let me tell you, I will never regret time spent with my kids. I will never regret being there for them. But looking back now, I probably, at the very least, would carve out some time for a jog a few days a week if I had to do it all over again.

And, I really couldn't complete this chapter without talking about guilt regarding friends. The problem here is that I spent so much time feeling guilt towards my kids AND feeling guilt towards my friends. When, out of guilt, I started retreating from the real world in order to focus on my kids, I essentially abandoned my friends. And then felt guilty about that. I just didn't have the time or energy or money to be a full time mom and a full time friend. So I started turning down offers to hang out with friends and, over time, the offers dwindled. I felt really bad about turning friends down. I knew I was not being an attentive friend. And I knew that I was running the risk of losing some friends because I turned down their offers or cancelled plans. But, here's the thing, if I had to do it all over again, I would do it exactly the same. I would choose my kids over my friends again and again. My kids will always be first. And yes, like I said before, I would probably modify things a little and give myself a little more freedom if I were doing this all again. I would probably try harder to make a girls' night out every once in a while. But, in a pinch, I would always choose my kids first.

So many situations have come and gone where I thought I needed to show my kids that I was enough. I needed to prove to them that I could compete with other moms and dads and that I was just as good. I thought I was hurting them if I was not giving them everything. I thought I was hurting them if I was not perfect. I was sure they would be scarred for life if I let them miss out on anything that the other kids were doing. I was convinced that I was hurting them if all I had to offer them was my love. And this caused mounds of guilt and so much energy wasted on bad feelings. I now know that I was wrong. My kids love me because, if nothing else, I am their mom. They love me for me. They love the time we spend together. They see how much I love them. And I shouldn't feel guilty for not having the same paycheck as

Margaret down the street. And I shouldn't feel guilty for going to dinner with my girlfriends once a month. And I shouldn't feel guilty for wanting to take care of my body by going for a jog.

Guilt is so debilitating and so stunting and sometimes so unfounded. I love my kids more than anything and they know that. If I could do things over, I would probably give way less energy to guilty feelings and spend more time just loving my babies. For so long I didn't even realize that it was guilt I was feeling.

Anyway. Here's what I have learned about guilt:

1. Feeling guilty does not always mean that you are, in fact, guilty. I mean seriously. If I put an orange in my daughter's lunch instead of an apple, what am I guilty of? I wouldn't think that this would qualify as child abuse or something equally horrible. And if I am not absolutely perfect 100% of the time? I am pretty sure that doesn't make me guilty of anything but being human.

2. Guilty feelings are useless. I am serious. I mean, unless you really did commit some terrible crime or did something actually bad, guilty feelings are not necessary. It's my personal opinion that guilty feelings inflict more harm than good. Guilty feelings can be debilitating and really do a number on your self-esteem. Yuck.

3. The things you lose sleep over because you feel so guilty about them have probably not even really mattered to your kids. Slipped an orange in her lunch because you were out of apples? She probably pouted for like twelve seconds and then moved on. And she still loves you more than anything. Accidentally forgot to pack your son's baseball in his school bag? He probably likes the ones they have at school better anyway. Had to cancel your plans to go on the field trip to the zoo because you got trapped at work? Your kids probably didn't want you to tag along anyway!

4. Here's the truth. You may lose some friends along the way. You may have people that don't understand your choices. There may be people who just cannot relate to your single parent life. When all you have the time and energy and money for is you and your kids, that's okay! There is only so much you can give until you are completely drained. If your friends really care about you, they will be there ready and waiting for you when you do decide you are ready for that night out. And, if you choose to put your kids before anyone else, I don't think you will ever regret that.

If you are a struggling mom or dad who's feeling like you just can't compete, I hope you will stop for just a minute and acknowledge that the fact alone that you are so concerned about your kids' feelings means you are most likely doing a really good job. The fact that you put any thought into whether or not your actions will have consequences that affect your kids means that you are way ahead of some parents. You are allowed to have a minute to yourself without guilt. You are allowed to

sometimes put an orange in your daughter's
lunch instead of an apple and not feel guilty.
You are allowed to let go of the guilt and just be
your freaking self.

Chapter 4: *Party of Three*

I t was a beautiful evening. The kids and I had spent the day exploring the beach and we were tanned and tired and looking forward to a great dinner. It was summer vacation and the three of us were on a cruise in the Caribbean.

We showered in our cabin, got dressed, and headed to the dining room. The fancy maître d' greeted us and said, "How many please?"

I replied, "Just three thanks."

He replied, "Your husband won't be joining us this evening?"

Hmmmmm. No sir, he won't. He won't be joining us this evening because he doesn't exist.

My kids and I have had this happen multiple times now. And at first it was horribly awkward and my immediate thought was that my kids would be suffering some sort of devastating, irreparable trauma and that I was a horrible person for taking them out among the public and exposing them to such torture.

But after having happened several times, it has now become an inside joke between us and we just laugh when it happens. My daughter will turn to me and say, "Yeah mom, will he be joining us?" and we will burst out laughing. Maybe one day he really will show up at dinner. Who knows?

This is just another one of the perks of single parenting. Being an odd number. Literally and figuratively. When the three of us travel together, go to dinner together, or whatever else, it SEEMS like we are the only ones without an "intact" family. It FEELS like we are the odd ones. All the other families have a mommy and daddy. It almost feels like we are broken or something, or at the very least like we are different from everyone else.

And seriously, it's so much easier to travel, go to the grocery store, go to a football game or whatever when there are two parents together. I mean I am sure we can all agree that taking multiple kids to Disneyworld is really not something that a single parent longs to do alone. If you will, please just imagine navigating trips to the bathroom, two-person rides, and lunch breaks with just you and your kids. Eek. And what do you do when you go to a stadium for a football game, trek all the way to your nosebleed seats, get settled, and one kid says that they need to go to the bathroom? And the other kid insists that there is absolutely no freaking way they are leaving their seat? Lord, give me strength. When there is just one of you, this type of thing gets old really quick.

This takes some getting used to. I have always been consumed with concern about the damage my kids may endure thanks to their dad and me getting divorced. One thing I was always worried about was whether it would make them feel different from the other kids. I never wanted them to feel ashamed or embarrassed by their parents. Although, now that I have teenagers, I know that there is no avoiding that…

I know firsthand, as anyone who has survived their teenage years knows, that when you are a teenager you will do almost anything to be seen as "normal". Your biggest fear is being seen as weird or different. When I was just 14, my mom passed away after a battle with cancer. Well, needless to say, this made me feel really different from almost all of the other kids at school. I felt really awkward and totally abnormal. So, in an effort to avoid complete awkwardness and possible rejection, on several occasions when I met someone new who didn't know anything about me, I lied to them and acted like I had a totally normal home and my mom was alive and well. I pretended that she was at home cooking dinner. I know, I know. When I think about this now, I cringe. But I also feel sad for that little girl and I am reminded that I don't want my kids to ever feel that way. I don't want them to feel like they are so incredibly different that they need to lie and hide the truth.

If you have kids and you get divorced, there's a never-ending stream of opportunities to point out your brokenness. Whose name and address goes on the emergency forms? Who gets called first when there is a problem at school? Who takes the dog to the vet? Who even gets the dog?

Getting divorced automatically thrusts the kids into two single-parent households and automatically thrusts each parent into the head of the household role. So when you are spending time with the kids, you feel the brokenness and when you are alone you feel the brokenness as well.

And becoming a single parent definitely does not only affect things involving the kids. One of the things I miss most about being married is when you leave a party and you and your spouse get in the car and then, on the ride home, the two of you talk about everybody at the party. That sounds so horrible and I don't really mean talking about people in a bad way. I mean, like, "Jim Bob is so funny!" "Carol is so sweet and quiet! She probably has a stripper pole in her bedroom," and "Debra said they decided they are going to homeschool all 17 of their kids? Holy crap, thank God it's her and not me!"

And you know how, when you are close to someone and think the same way, you can just look at the other person across the room and you just know what you both are thinking. It's like you have little inside jokes wherever you go. It's like you are a little team of two taking on the world. I miss that. I miss having someone to deconstruct an entire cocktail party's worth of conversations with on the ride home; when you are by yourself, you kind of wonder if your interpretations are true. With nobody to back you up, you are not always sure. And for real, it is so nice to have another person to help you get out of situations when you are ready to go home, put your pajamas on, and go to bed. I mean you can't deny how refreshing it is to have a partner that will go to the bathroom and call your phone so that you can claim that the babysitter is calling and you need to head out. And then when they come out of the bathroom, you can act all disappointed and say, "Well, this really sucks so bad and I hate to say it but the sitter just called and Tommy has thrown up twice so we have to leave now." Then you can both act all disappointed and say your goodbyes and head for the door. And, if you are really lucky, you can get ice cream on the way home.

When you are married, you don't realize how pronounced your singleness will be when you become single. Nobody to help with the groceries. Nobody to help with putting the kids to bed. Nobody to go to the movies with. Nobody to discuss the light bill with. Nobody to freak out with when the principal's office calls. Nobody to yell at the kids when you are just too damn exhausted to do it.

And for some reason, this one here has always hit me the hardest. Nobody to put for an emergency contact when you are filling out paperwork of whatever kind. The first time I went to the doctor after getting divorced, I was filling out forms and reached the emergency contact section. Who should I put? I wound up putting either my brother or dad but I always felt really awkward about that. Like I am a 45-year-old woman and my emergency contact is my dad? Talk about humbling. I felt unclaimed. I know, it's ridiculous.

As far as raising kids goes, I really operate better in a team setting to be honest. This is because I am a huge pushover. I mean really huge pushover.

"Mom, will you wake up two hours earlier and make me eggs Benedict for breakfast?"

"Absolutely!"

"Mom, will you get out of bed and come upstairs and hand me my phone that is on the table only two feet away from me?"

"Be right there!"

"Mom, will you give me $75,000 to buy this cool bike I want?"

"Of course, let me just go sell one of my kidneys. Be right back!"

Anyway, I am always better at parenting and discipline when I have some backup. Someone to side with me, agree with me, and present a team front to the kids with me. Like a hype man. I need a parenting hype man. Someone to stand behind me when I am attempting to discipline or set boundaries. Someone in the background yelling, "You go, girl! Tell them no like you mean it!" "Hell yeah, you show them what serious looks like!" "You two better listen to your momma! OR ELSE!"

It is also massively helpful to have someone to just be in the house. I used to be able to run out to the mailbox with no worries because my husband would be inside with the kids. I could take a bubble bath and completely relax because someone else was in charge. I could go to the grocery store ALONE because my husband would be at home with the kids. I could rest peacefully knowing that, if our house caught fire, at least there were two of us to rescue the kids. When you become a single parent, all of these things have to be strategically planned. Since becoming a single parent I have on multiple occasions lain awake at night planning my and my kids' emergency exit plan with great detail. And, more times than I can count, I have prayed to the good Lord above that nothing terrible happens while I take a really quick shower. Or I have wished on a lucky star that the house doesn't burn down with my kids inside while I run out to the mailbox. And I am not ashamed to say that, for a good bit of time, the daycare at my gym was my favorite babysitter. I could have a solid hour of freedom in which I could work out, sit and drink coffee with my girlfriend, or go sit in the sun by the pool and take a freaking nap.

It's especially good to be part of a team, I have found, when it comes to anything related to school. Let's say your daughter has a soccer game. Nobody else, and I mean nobody, is going to cheer as strongly as you or get as worked up as you as the other parent. Besides your daughter's other parent, who else is going to make a complete fool of themselves with all that cheering? Who else is going to talk smack about that little brat Emily who always steals the ball? Who else is going to, right along with you, want to punch the coach in the throat for that thing he said that made you pissed? And that's just soccer! I cannot even begin to say how seriously necessary it feels to have a teammate when you are sitting in the principal's office. Ugh. I mean you really need backup there. And you really need someone with whom you can rehash the entire meeting afterwards. When you go to the principal's office, a major debriefing and reassessment is totally required afterwards. And even if you are not on the best terms with your partner, just having a warm body sitting next to you is mentally empowering, some other soul that equally believes in your kid and will equally do what's necessary to fight to keep them in school.

And it would take me way too long to talk about how it feels to be the one different family at friend and family gatherings like Christmas or birthdays or whatever. It always makes me think of that song, "Which of these things is not like the others?"

So, to be honest, this is all one part of being a single-parent family that you really can't escape. There's not a whole lot of advice I can think of unless you want to move to Antarctica and never interact with other humans again, which, come to think of it, sounds kind of appealing sometimes. Anyway, things I have learned about this are:

1. We are definitely not, even though it really, really feels like it sometimes, the only divorced family in town. Remember, Wikipedia already told us there are plenty of others. And even if I don't personally know them, they do exist. And even if we were the only divorced family in this town, that wouldn't be unusual because it is quite a small town. But I would imagine that, most definitely, the next town over has another divorced family.

2. In an effort to look at the bright side, I need to try to remember that divorce is by no means the absolute worst thing that could happen to me and my kids. There are by far way worse things. And as long as I am trying my hardest and doing my best and giving out a crazy amount of love and hugs

and kisses, everything will probably be just
fine. And maybe even way better than fine.

3. When I am feeling different than everyone
    else and like I just wish we were a "normal"
    family, I need to consider this: someone I
    know (or maybe don't know) may be
    wishing and praying for exactly what I have
    right now. There may be a husband I know
    that is trapped in an abusive relationship and
    would give anything to be free from it with
    just him and his kids. There may be a single
    woman somewhere who has never been
    married and is unable to have kids of her
    own and would give her right arm to have
    two beautiful children and couldn't care less
    if she ever gets married or not. When I really
    think about it, I am so darn blessed and
    things could be so much worse.

4. The fact of the matter is that, unfortunately,
    there are going to be scenarios that I just
    can't avoid since becoming a single parent.
    Graduations, weddings, life events. All I can
    do in these situations is put on my big girl

panties and deal with it. Put on my Sunday best, hold my head high, and march my brave self right into that auditorium or wherever. Hold myself together, act like I am the most confident person in the room, and smile like nobody's business. Lead by example for my kids. And then, when it's over, go home and cry if I need to. Or eat a dozen donuts. Or whatever does the trick.

Being a single parent adds a level of responsibility and aloneness that is sometimes overwhelming. I have felt a loneliness that I didn't know was possible at times. I have felt overly stressed about simple things and blown my fears way out of proportion because I felt so alone. But it definitely gets better with time. And I definitely don't feel so different anymore. And, quite frankly, who really gives a flip if I am?

Chapter 5: *Decisions*

I have a track record of NOT being the best decision maker. I once saw a T-shirt that said, "I am just going to wing it," and in small print underneath, it said, "-me, about something I should most definitely not wing." That basically sums it up. Or better yet, the T-shirt that says, "My decision-making skills closely resemble those of a squirrel trying to cross the street.'' Exactly. Story of my life. I also have blonde hair and have been known, on occasion, to have very blonde moments.

I once thought it was a good idea to date a guy whose ex-wife still slept over on occasion. No big deal, she did it "for the kids." I once thought it would be a good idea to take out a payday loan to pay off a couple of bills. Seems like a legit financial plan. I once thought I would actually be successful at going on a ten-day liquid-only diet. Sounded like a practical, long-term plan.

I don't like making decisions. I typically avoid them when I can. I mean I actually avoid them at all costs. That is something I absolutely miss about being married, the ability to defer decisions to another human being. The problem with decisions is that, if you make the decision, then you are, by default, responsible for the consequences of that decision. So, I would just rather not participate. If you decide what to make for dinner and the family doesn't like it, you have to hear about it. If you decide what stocks to purchase and they tank, you lose all your money. If you decide to take the "back way", you have to live with the consequences if you end up in Albuquerque. If you decide to have just one more drink, you probably will wake up in the front yard. The list is endless.

One day, I was at home alone trying to figure out what to do because my to-do list was eight miles long. My kids were not home and I had some free time. *Should I cut the grass? Should I wash the dog? Should I go for a walk? Should I pay bills? Should I do laundry? Should I catch up on paperwork for my job? Should I eat?* I stood in the hallway for half a second and realized I was shaking. Literally shaking. I didn't know why. I stood in the hallway thinking about this for just a minute and then figured I must be hungry and moved on to the kitchen to make lunch.

That night, I got in bed and watched a movie (*I can only imagine* —that MercyMe movie, which is INCREDIBLE!) and cried my way through the whole movie. The movie was sad in parts so crying was appropriate. But the thing is I was bawling. Like full-blown sobbing. Like my nose was running all over the place and my eyes were puffy and red and my face hurt from being scrunched up. The whole entire movie! Anyway, I went to sleep and that night I woke up at around 4:00 a.m. because the neighbor's dog was barking. In the darkness, it hit me. I had been shaking and crying the day before because I was terrified. I was scared to death. I was living in absolute fear.

For several weeks, I had been trying to decide if I would let my house foreclose, try to sell it fast, or file bankruptcy. And I was trying to make these decisions all on my own. Nobody knew. Not even my kids. Just me. Massive life decisions and the responsibility were all on me. I had to make the right choices. I had to figure it out. Nobody to walk with me through this. Nobody to calm me down if I freaked out. Nobody to bounce my ideas off of. Nobody to help me research the choices. Nobody to stay up late at night with and talk it through. Nobody to help me carry the burden. Nobody to be devastated right along with me. Just me.

I sat in the darkness and really thought about this. For years, at this point, I had been making decisions, big and small, all alone. That's a huge responsibility. That's mounds of stress and especially when you are constantly in motion and trying to get everything done. You may not actually realize everything that you really are dealing with. Who has time to stop and think about all you have been through when you are just going and going and going? This is not to say that I have not had down time, but I just had never really acknowledged that one of the facets of being a single parent is the responsibility of making all of the decisions on your own. I let it get to the point where it literally stopped me in my tracks and I had to acknowledge it.

Several months before this moment, my car broke down. I got it fixed. And then it broke down again. This was so irritating but not the end of the world. But I had reached the point where I needed to make a decision. I needed to choose whether or not I should fix it or just go ahead and get a new car. I couldn't figure out what to do. I wanted so badly to make the RIGHT decision. I put mounds of pressure on myself to figure it out. It was exhausting. And honestly, I think it was the start of my slow descent into decision burnout. I found myself in one situation after another where I had to make a big decision and I was getting more and more frustrated and exhausted. I don't even know if decision burnout is a real thing, but it sure felt like it to me.

Not only are you making thousands of big and small decisions over time, but, oftentimes, you are making them in a split second. Can Tommy have a sleepover? Can I sit in the front seat? Can I have a Dr. Pepper? Can I hold the kitten? Can I go over to Susie's house? Can I stay up late tonight? Can I go home with Jimmy after school? Most of these types of questions require a quick response, which, when you have 872,311 things on your mind, can be a little stressful.

Quite frankly, even making small decisions alone becomes burdensome after some time. Choosing what to have for dinner every single night, choosing what to do for the weekend, choosing what your kids' curfew should be, choosing if you should punish them for coming home six minutes late, choosing if you should cut the grass today or tomorrow, choosing if you should get the oil changed in the car or let it go 500 more miles (or 5000?), etc., etc., etc. It all adds up over time. It's cumulative.

Over the last year or so, I have been dreaming of taking a vacation where I don't have to make any decisions. Seriously. I daydream about it. Like someone emails me a non-negotiable itinerary and I get on a plane (or boat, or whatever) and take off for a week. I imagine it would be like an all-inclusive resort or something in a beautiful place and probably on an exotic beach. But the most outstanding feature is that I don't have to make a single decision. I follow the itinerary, eat the food I am served, and completely shut my brain down. I don't have to think or figure out a single thing. Sounds like heaven to me.

I do miss that about being married. Love them or hate them, at least when you are married, you have another human being to share the decision-making with you. Someone else to help you, at least some of the time, decide what to make for dinner.

And I should also stop here for a second and acknowledge the fact that I have always had people that I COULD ask for help or advice or whatever. I have an incredible brother and sister-in-law and other family, incredible friends, and incredible coworkers. But one of my (many) faults is my inability to speak up and ask for help, especially when it comes to personal matters. I have a hang up about dishing out personal, and sometimes embarrassing, information for others to dissect. And I am one of those weirdos that gets stressed by the thought of "burdening" others with my problems. And really I would not recommend that you operate like I have in the past. Seriously. If you never let other people know about your problems or reach out and ask for help, it will 100% come back to bite you in the ass.

It's like being on a sinking boat and having a little tiny bucket and trying to get the water out. The whole time you are sinking you don't yell for help because you are darn sure that you've got this and you can get all of that water out all by yourself. And then you keep going down. And the water keeps coming in. And just when you realize that maybe you don't have this and maybe you could use some help, you scream for help just as your head goes under water. If I would have asked for help or advice a lot earlier, I may never have been in a situation where I was trying to choose between foreclosure, bankruptcy, or homelessness. If I would have spoken up and asked for help, I am sure my brother would have helped me fix my car. I am sure if I put my pride aside and said I needed a hand with anything, there are a bunch of people that would have jumped to help me.

So here are some things I have learned about single-parent decision-making:

1. Even if I am absolutely, 100% sure that I am all alone in this, I most probably am not! Even if the thought of reaching out to Aunt Sue for help with my taxes makes me want to gouge my eyes out, I should just do it! She probably really would love to help and even if she gives me hell about not keeping track of my charitable donations, I should just smile and agree and then take myself for a night out with all that time and money she saved me. And here's a pro tip to myself from an expert (me) on this matter: don't let all my problems spiral too far out of control before I speak up. No, really. That leak in my roof needs fixing and I know my cousin could fix it but I hate to ask? Just ask

already! Do it before I need to ask him to replace all the sheet rock and flooring also because it flooded. Can't figure out how to file an extension on my taxes but I know my sister-in-law is a wizard at this and would totally love to help? Call her now! Do it before the IRS is garnishing my wages! I promise that the temporary pain of sucking it up and asking for help is minor in comparison to the disaster of letting things get out of control.

2. Okay, I am going to do it. I am going to talk about how beneficial meditation can be for calming my brain and making things seem manageable. I know this to be true because I was a skeptic and then I tried it and now I am a BELIEVER! A while back, I started meditating every morning for just a few minutes. And, without making a single other change, I started feeling better within a month or so. Decisions didn't intimidate me. I felt calm and fully equipped to take on whatever came at me. And I don't have documentation of this, but I swear that

stressful things stopped happening as frequently. I swear! Anyway, I believe in it.

3. Even when it really seems like it, every decision I make is not a life or death decision. It often feels like it is but it's really not. Sometimes it feels like if I don't make the exact perfect decision about something, my whole life will fall apart. I would argue that this is probably not true. I would argue that a lot of the time, no matter which decision I make, everything can and will work out. Deciding whether or not to take that new job? Honestly, my life will probably be just fine either way. I have not heard of too many people on their deathbed saying that they wished they would have taken that office assistant position with good benefits thirty years ago. I mean maybe. But I doubt it. And as far as my car goes, whether I had chosen to fix it or sell it, everything probably would have worked out about the same. I would be just fine either way. So I should try not to sweat it too much. It's all going to work out.

If you are a single momma or daddy, please stop for just one second and acknowledge the responsibility you have. Just acknowledge that you have survived up until today making decisions all alone. Please give yourself some credit for making trillions of big and small decisions that should probably, in most cases, be two-person decisions. That's kind of a big deal.

Chapter 6: *If You Mess with My Kids, I Will Cut You*

L et's just talk for one quick minute about the idea of your ex introducing your kids to their new "love interest". Maybe other people are really good at dealing with this. And maybe they welcome, with open arms, a new person into their lives with not a moment's hesitation.

Maybe they instantly bond with the new girlfriend (or boyfriend) and start going for coffee next week or meeting at the gym for yoga. Maybe they start making synced calendars and planning coordinated holidays and using one big group text message. Maybe they even plan vacations together (are you kidding me right now?).

First of all, if you are like the person I just described above, you are AMAZING! You are a superhero. I could learn so much from you. And the world needs more people like you! I am, frankly, a bit jealous.

And maybe you are a single parent but have not yet had to endure this special kind of torture for whatever reason. If so, you may want to skip this chapter. Or, better yet, keep reading for a preview of what exciting things may be to come!

I am not the person described above. Not even close. Of course, I can be polite and cordial and not cause a scene. And I can put on my big girl panties and make small talk. And I can keep a smile on my face even when I want to punch someone. And the fact that I absolutely detest confrontation and don't like uncomfortable situations comes in handy here. But don't push it.

The first time I was introduced to my ex-husband's girlfriend (now wife) we were at the school fair. Let me just start by saying that my very first thought was, *What is she doing at the school fair?* Anyway, I did not know she would be there and that was problem number one. Thankfully, I saw them from a distance first and had a second to recover from shock before having to speak to them. And I am pretty sure I threw up in my mouth just a little.

First of all, this was the annual school fair which occurs towards the of end of the school year. And we live in south Louisiana which means late April can feel pretty much like a sauna outside on most days. So I was probably looking and feeling pretty sweaty and disheveled at this point anyway. And then I saw her. From a pretty good distance, coming around one of the school walkways, I saw my ex husband walking with someone. And, okay I will be completely honest. My very first thought was, *Who's that little girl with him?* Ouch. So after about 15 seconds of squinting in the glaring sunshine and trying to figure out who she was, it hit me. IT WAS HER! I stood there for a few more seconds staring. I felt frozen and like I couldn't breath. I was not prepared for this! I immediately started sweating even more and slightly shaking. Thankfully my kids were off running around with their friends and I was by myself. I ducked in the nearest bathroom and hid in a stall while I came up with a plan. The only two options I could come up with were to either book the next flight out for Monrovia or to pull myself together and act like a big girl. Ugh. I REALLY wanted to choose the option that involved leaving the country. But, after an unnatural amount of time in the bathroom stall, I splashed some cold water on my face and did what I had to do.

I decided I would be courageous and approach them and introduce myself. It was massively awkward, but I said hello and introduced myself. We had an awkward and uncomfortable exchange about the beautiful weather or whatever and then I made myself scarce. It was done! I felt like a superhero! I had been brave, introduced myself, been polite, and SURVIVED! And, as obnoxious as this sounds,

I felt like I had won because I had approached them first and been friendly. Oy vey.

One thing's for sure, it's all fun and games until things get serious. Dad's gone on a few dates? No big deal. Good for him. Dad took the kids to dinner and introduced them to his girlfriend? Okay, that sounds nice. Dad can't take the kids next weekend because he is going to be out of town with his girlfriend? Um, okay. That's cool. Dad's girlfriend is taking the kids shopping while he is at work? Hmmmm. Dad has to go on a work trip on his weekend to have the kids, but he says they can stay with his girlfriend anyway? What!?!?! Okay, pump the brakes. Things are moving a little fast here, buckaroo. Let's just slow down here a minute. I have a few questions...

Has a proper background check been done on this person? Does she have a valid driver's license? Does she have a criminal record? Is she certified in CPR? Is she kind to little old ladies? Is she registered to vote? Does she know what to do in an emergency? What are her thoughts on global warming?

This is the point in time when things got a little messy for me. I guess my momma instinct kicked in or something. I started to feel slightly jealous and completely insecure. I did not see this coming. I started comparing myself to her even though I didn't know her. It had nothing to do with my ex-husband and everything to do with my kids. As far as I was concerned, she could have my ex-husband, but I wanted my kids all to myself. Selfish? Maybe. Childish? Probably. Ridiculous? Of course. But that's how I felt. And things in this department started going downhill quickly. Unfortunately, this is about the time when I descended into the nightmare of stalking. No worries, not REAL stalking. But Facebook, Instagram, Pinterest type stalking. Ugh. It felt so bad, but I wanted to know who this person was and, obviously, if she was better than me. Would my kids love her more than me?

I was ashamed and kept all of these fears and feelings to myself. None of my friends were in the same situation as I was so I thought it might be a little awkward to discuss.

"Oh hey girl, what have you been up to?"

"Oh, you know, not much, just spent the last three and a half hours in my pajamas browsing my ex-husband's girlfriend's bedroom board on Pinterest. You know, the usual."

So embarrassing. But whatever.

I started drastically jumping to conclusions about her. She probably cooks all organic, vegan food for every meal. She probably wears an apron. She probably snapchats. She probably has an unnatural amount of patience. She probably makes organic, homemade dog food. She probably meditates every morning for two hours. She probably buys presents for my kids that they love and that I can't afford. She probably has a good hair day every single day. She probably brushes my daughter's hair every night as they bond. She probably rides bikes with my son and she can probably do a wheelie. She probably already got them for Christmas every single item on their Christmas list. She probably wakes up early every morning to make them a hearty breakfast before school instead of frozen waffles. She probably hand washes their clothes with non-toxic soap and essential oils. She probably is PERFECT.

Now, I can't speak for guys on this because I honestly don't know if they even think this way. I mean do they? Maybe they just make friends with the new guy and call it a day. Maybe they are instant BFFs and start hanging out together at the bar on Tuesdays. Maybe they meet up at the gym and start planning their fantasy football picks.

Or maybe they think just like girls but in their own kind of way. Like... That guy probably deadlifts like nobody's business. That guy probably has a riding lawn mower. That guy probably goes to the gym at 3:00 a.m. and blasts out 40 sets of bench presses before the sun even comes up. That guy probably has an ex-girlfriend that looks like Jennifer Anniston. That guy is probably hung like a mule.

Anyway, for me the list went on and on and spiraled out of control. How embarrassing. I was absolutely certain that my kids were madly in love with this woman and would probably come home one day and pack their bags and announce that they were riding off into the sunset with her. I was fully convinced that she was a way better human than I could ever be.

It took me some time, and a little pouting, to move past this. It really did have an impact on my self-esteem. And for a while I lived with a fear of missing out. What if my son fell off his bike and she was the one to comfort him? What if my daughter came home from school crying and she was the one who got to talk to her about it? What if they chose to talk to her about their problems instead of me?

I might also add that it was around this time that I started feeling really stressed out. I had to work way more hours to make ends meet, I had less time to exercise, and I just felt like the whole world was on my shoulders. This was a low time for me. I was cranky, tired, and not feeling it. And my self-esteem plummeted. The side effect of all of this? I gained 30 pounds. Thirty!!!! In just one year. And I felt horrible. Physically and mentally. The reason I am mentioning this here is because, with my newly gained 30 pounds, I officially felt like the stereotypical frumpy ex-wife. Ugh. This only fueled my insecurity and my belief that my kids would fall out of love with me and into love with her. For most of my adult life leading up to this time, I had been active. I ran marathons, did triathlons, and exercised religiously. So this new heavy body was bordering on traumatic for me. I was convinced that I was a complete failure in life.

This was about the time that I really cut myself off from the world for a while. I only worked, spent time with the kids, ate, and slept. Nothing much else. I felt ashamed of myself and started feeling embarrassed to go out in public. So I started turning down invitations to get-togethers or anything else that involved mingling or meeting people. Food really was my friend during this time. And I felt miserable. My self-esteem took a nosedive. And, as usual, I beat myself up for feeling miserable about this. After finishing off some donuts or cookies, I would look in the mirror and feel so bad about myself and was absolutely certain that this other woman would never do such a disgusting thing. I would fall into a serious shame spiral. Of course my kids would love her more than me! Her with her cute little figure versus me with my frumpy old mom figure. I was sure she probably had all kinds of self-discipline and self-love. I literally had zero.

Unfortunately, there always comes a time when, eventually, you are forced to come face-to-face with the person or people you want so badly to avoid. Having kids together with someone generally means that for the REST OF YOUR LIFE there will be endless opportunities for reuniting—soccer games, graduations, principal's offices, recitals, weddings, funerals, etc., etc., etc. And if you have ever had to endure the massively awkward situations when you are put in the same room together, you will know what it feels like to want to run for your life. Like where do I sit? Do I say hello casually? Do we hug? Do we ignore each other? Do I take this opportunity to punch her face? Do I act like we are old friends? Do I just stare at my phone and act like I am consumed with some important business matter? Do we all sit together like one big happy family? Do we sit separately? Do the kids sit with me? Do the kids sit with him? Ugh, the list goes on forever. And it's one thing to be looking good and feeling good while having to co-mingle, but when you have gained thirty pounds, feel yucky, and your self-esteem is shot, you typically dread these kinds of situations.

I used to daydream about losing weight and getting into the best shape of my life. I would win the lottery, get a super hunky boyfriend, and get a whole new wardrobe. I would get my best haircut ever and then casually show up to the school play like I owned the world. I would act cool while their jaws dropped and they instantly felt jealous, insecure, and lacking. Yeah, well, that never happened.

I sulked quietly about this to myself for quite some time. And, honestly, it took me quite a few episodes of pouting, bad attitude, and pretty much being a big baby before I decided to pull it together. But eventually it passed, and I realized that my kids still loved me and I was still their momma. I really did realize that, no matter what, they would not stop loving and adoring me just because she was in their life now.

The crazy thing is, for a while I wanted her to be a bad person because then my kids would not like her more than me. I wanted her to have faults. I wanted my kids to run home to me and tell me how mean she was. And, to be completely honest, there were many times when it would have made my day if my kids had come home and said she had caught some rare virus that caused her to grow four heads and sixteen eyeballs and because of this my kids were scared of her and would never go near her again! I know; it's so mean. But that was my lovely insecurity for you.

Of course I want someone who adores my kids and is kind to them. I want someone who treats them like they would treat their own kids. And I want her to be a genuinely good human. And, as much as I used to hate to admit it, I do believe that my kids' stepmom is a genuinely good human and treats my kids well. I think she is loving to them. And I think she cares about them and wants the best for them. And I am so thankful for that. What a blessing. I absolutely cannot imagine if I were in a situation where my kids' stepmom was a shady character or I knew she treated them poorly. Lord help her because I would probably need bail money if that were the case.

And, honestly, I still have moments when I feel jealous and insecure about the whole situation. As every milestone comes and goes, I am reminded that I am not the only woman in my kids' lives. I am reminded that I have to share. And the truth is that really hurts. It is certainly not what I dreamed of when my kids were babies. I never imagined I would be sharing the two most important people in my life with someone I did not choose or come to know and trust.

And I should mention that I find it to be such an odd thing that my kids have family in their life that I don't even know and have never met. No really. It's like my own two children have a whole other life that I am not a part of. And that is a really, really weird feeling to me. My kids' stepmom obviously has her own family and this family is now my kids' family. But not mine. They, I would imagine, get together for holidays, celebrate birthdays, and share lives. They do normal family things. And even if my kids were to fill me in on stuff about their family, it's not the same as if I knew them. It's like my kids are leading two separate lives and, on some level, that has got to feel weird to them and maybe even uncomfortable.

When I was newly divorced and still naively unaware of all the things that could possibly be ahead in my new single mom life, one thing I really did not consider was the possibility of my ex-husband having more children. Nope, the thought had not even entered my mind. Not at all. I mean he already has the two most awesome kids around, right? Well, cut to a few years later when I find out accidentally through a mutual friend that my ex-husband and his new wife are expecting. Say what! Expecting a baby? Holy cannoli. I need to sit down.

Now, here's the thing. It's not that I really was upset by this news. I just really hadn't thought about it. And I had long since gotten over any weird feelings about their relationship. No, this was more of a shock in relation to the idea that my kids were going to have a little brother or sister and I was not going to be the mother. This felt really hard for me to wrap my head around. Kind of disorienting. Like let's say this baby is a girl. When I ask my son, "Where's your sister?" will he know which one I am talking about? Will there be confusion? Because, honestly, if I am not living with and raising this baby, I may from time to time forget that she exists. And I very honestly mean this with no ill will. It's just that, obviously, when you are not living with someone 24/7, you aren't really thinking about them constantly like the people you actually live with. But, for all future reference, if I ask him about his sister, I am 99.999% most likely talking about the sister that I birthed, not the one that lives a few miles away and I have never met. How awkward.

Anyway, my kids will always be my kids and I will always love and support them. And I will try my hardest to be open-minded and supportive when it comes to matters involving their dad and stepmom and new sibling. So, here are the lessons that I have learned (the hard way, of course) in regards to "new friends" in my kids' lives:

1. My kids will always love me simply because I am their mommy. Yep. They really will! I don't have to compete with anyone else or get concerned that another woman will win them over and ride off into the sunset with them. Sure, they will have moments when they are feeling the love for her and I may feel some little twinges of jealousy. But, in the end, they will always come home to me.

Despite all my faults and hang-ups, they won't quit loving me.

2. Sharing is caring. Ugh, I know. As much as this has, in the past, been a super hard thing for me to admit, allowing my kids the freedom to have a relationship with their stepmom really is the right thing to do. And, please don't get me wrong, this has been SO HARD for me. And I have had my fair share of pouty, jealous moments about this. And I have secretly wished, more times than I want to admit, that my kids would find some major faults in their stepmom and reject her. But I now know that that is not in their best interest. I know it is beneficial to them to have nothing but loving and supportive relationships. Even when it's hard for me to swallow. And when I think of the possible alternatives, I have to be so grateful that my kids have a stepmom who loves them.

3. My children's dad and stepmom aren't going anywhere anytime soon so I may as

well suck it up and get on the bandwagon. As much as I want to be the lead role in my kids' lives, I have to let that idea go. And I can choose to either pout about it for all of eternity or I can act like a mature grown-up and be supportive. It doesn't serve anyone to have a bad attitude about it. And do I really want to spend the rest of my life playing the role of the frumpy, bitter, jealous, angry ex-wife? NO WAY! I've got a big, exciting life ahead of me and negative vibes don't fit into that picture. And I do not want to bring my kids down or cause them to resent me and, believe it or not, being negative Nancy WILL bring them down. And do I really want to add to their list of things that they are going to need to talk to a therapist about? Do I really want them telling a therapist that I was bitter, controlling, and pouty? No freaking way.

So, to sum things up, my kids love me and they love their dad and stepmom and that's that. End of story. Our relationships are still a work in progress and there is a lot left to be desired, but we are headed in the right direction. And although in the past I have feared that my kids would tragically fall out of love with me and madly in love with someone else, it has yet to happen. They love me. And I am now, and will always be, their momma. And if you mess with them, I will cut you.

Chapter 7: *Keeping My Mouth Shut*

There are certain things in life that I am good at. I am good at brushing my teeth twice, maybe three times a day. I am pretty good at making sure I get eight hours of sleep a night. I am really good at making grilled cheese sandwiches. I excel at avoiding confrontation. I am unbelievable at

Candy Crush. And I can start an IV like nobody's business.

But some things just don't come naturally to me. Beyond grilled cheese, I am pretty much useless in the kitchen. I don't typically do real well with setting boundaries or stating my needs. I am terrible at gardening and kill every single plant I touch. I probably can't name all fifty state capitals. I am a terrible singer. And I am the absolute worst at small talk.

And, unfortunately, I am terrible at keeping my mouth shut. That would be all fine and dandy except for the fact that I am a divorced single parent. Now, just by the fact alone that I am divorced, you can draw the conclusion that my ex-husband and I have not always been the best communicators. We probably haven't always had the nicest things to say to or about each other. There have been multiple occasions on which I have really had to zip my mouth shut and not say anything. And if we didn't have kids together I guess that would really not be a big deal. But we do have kids together. And, like most other parents I assume, I would prefer not to be responsible for scarring them for life.

Keeping my mouth shut has been like an Olympic sport to me since getting divorced. Oh, I can count soooooo many times when I had a whole lot I wanted to get off my chest. But, in the interest of my children's sanity, I exercised every single muscle in my face to keep my mouth shut. And, to be completely fair, I would venture to guess that my ex-husband has had a whole lot that he would like to get off his chest as well. Yikes.

And the fact of the matter is that it has become glaringly obvious to me that when I need to speak up, I typically don't, and when I need to shut up, I also typically don't. When I am overwhelmed and could use some help, I tend to say nothing. When I feel lost and hopeless, my mouth is zipped. When I feel like my boundaries are being crossed, go ahead and feel free to cross because chances are I will say nothing. But if someone on the interstate even slightly cuts me off or if my job asks me to work overtime or my ex-husband breathes (just kidding☺), then Lord help me. My mouth will be wide open and spewing anything and everything I have to say.

Regardless of whether you have children or not, divorce, in and of itself, is guaranteed to make a person want to get some things off their chest. I certainly am not aware of any divorcing couples that had nary a negative word to say about their ex. I would imagine that if you had only positive things to say about your ex, it could be questioned why you are even divorced at all.

What's really crazy is that after getting divorced the amount of things you have to work through and communicate about seems to INCREASE instead of decrease. Suddenly there are all kinds of things to work out and they can't really be avoided. Who will live where? Who will take the kids to school on which days? Who will take the dog to the vet? Who will get Aunt Martha's antique china cabinet? I mean I could go on and on. And the expectation is that both involved parties will remain calm and make all of these decisions in a fair and thoughtful manner. Seriously? I mean we are getting divorced after all. Clearly we weren't really good at communicating and working together to start with. And now I am supposed to be all peaceful and fair and polite? Ugh.

For example, imagine the following conversations taking place RIGHT in front of the kids:

Oh, you can't take the kids this weekend because you are going to Tahiti? *Okay girl, zip it.*

Oh, you think it's okay for the kids to have no curfew? *I know, I know, but you have to zip it.*

Oh, you want to take the kids to your girlfriend's parents' house in Antarctica for Thanksgiving? *ZIP IT NOW!!*

Anyway, the fact of the matter is that, as a newly divorced single parent, there are going to be multiple occasions on which you may wish to "speak your mind," if you know what I mean. My advice to anyone listening would be to zip it up. Yep, zip it up tight.

I thought about giving a few funny examples of times when I really had to force myself to keep my mouth shut over the past few years. Because believe me when I say there have been many. But then it occurred to me that I guess there's a slight little bit of a chance that my kids may read this one day. Oy vey.

So, instead of opening my mouth and potentially scarring my children any further, I will instead move straight ahead into my list of things I have learned about keeping my mouth shut. Here goes:

1. Just do it. No, really. It's as simple and utterly difficult as that. There have been just a handful of occasions over the years when I just couldn't hold it in and I said something negative to or about my children's dad in front of them. And I instantly regretted it every time. I felt like a complete selfish jerk. And even though on the eight million other occasions when I wanted to say something but forced myself to shut it up and felt really happy that I did, it was literally one of the hardest things I have ever had to do. In the heat of the moment, I was always sure that my ex-husband NEEDED to know what I had to say. And the thought of keeping it to myself was excruciating and it seemed like I might explode if I didn't get it out. But somehow I would succeed in keeping it in and, even though it felt absolutely horrible for a while and I thought I might die, in the

end I was always proud of myself for shutting up.

2. The things that I was so absolutely certain needed to be said and that I got so worked up about didn't really even matter after some time, even when I never got them off my chest. Imagine that. Sometimes I look back on things I got so upset about and I think to myself, *Jeez, what was the big deal? Who even cares?* Sometimes I can't even remember what I was mad about and that's crazy because at the time, when I was in the heat of the moment and all worked up, I was 100% certain I would NEVER get over whatever it was. Well, here we are a few years later and I can say that I am 100% over all of it. EVEN the things that I never got off my chest.

3. The experts are probably correct when they say that spewing negative drama in front of your kids probably does, unfortunately, screw them up more than would be preferable. So zipping it up really is the best

idea. I don't know any statistics or, honestly, facts about this, but I do know that I have heard this many times before and it just makes common sense. It can't possibly be beneficial to Timmy to hear his mom calling his dad a no-good loser. Even if it's true. And it can't possibly be a good thing for Missy to hear her dad repeatedly say that her mom is useless. Even if it's true. I 100% believe that if these statements are indeed correct, the kids will figure this stuff out on their own one day. So sit back, zip it up, and let time and karma work their magic.

4. There is literally no better feeling in the world than being proud of yourself for not being a screaming idiot. And after some time spent keeping your mouth shut it feels really freaking good to be able to say that you sucked it up and did the right thing. I mean choosing to make yourself really uncomfortable by keeping your thoughts to yourself in an effort to protect your kids is a ginormous accomplishment and deserves a major pat on the back. And it feels good! So zip it up!

If you are a single mom or dad and you are 100% absolutely certain that you have to get that absolutely horrible thing off your chest right now, STOP! Please! I promise that you will most likely regret it. And I promise you that if you keep your mouth shut, in the interest of your children, you will feel so good about it and the feeling will be so much better than the half second of gratification you would get from vomiting venom on your ex. Even if they deserve it.

Chapter 8: *Money (or lack thereof)*

Speaking of stress. Sweet baby Jesus. I have spent a large portion of my adult life trying to manage money. I have a history of being a better spender than saver. And I have probably spent way too much time feeling buyer's remorse. I seem to have been born with one of those attitudes that causes me to think to myself, *go ahead and take that vacation, you only live once!* Or, *look I could die at any time so why not go ahead and by those Super Bowl tickets?* Meanwhile, several weeks later I am kicking myself when I am still very much alive and have to pay the light bill.

Being in a couple, at least there are two people responsible for the finances. If Susie starts binge buying antiques, Bobby can rein her in. If Billy is dropping too many dollars at the local GNC, Emily can put a stop to it. Even if one person is designated as the person in charge, someone else is, at least, partially in the mix. There is at least another warm body that you have to be accountable to. When you are single, not another soul will be looking at your checking account balance.

When my ex-husband and I split up in 2012, I was a stay-at-home mom/nursing student at the time. I had no income. I had been a stay-at-home mom for the eleven previous years and had not worked since before my son was born. This meant that I had no income, no savings of my own, and no clue how I would survive. And yes, I was a full-time student in nursing school. So with being a full time mom and being a student, there was not a single available minute in my days. Definitely no time for a job.

At the time, we lived in a nice house in a nice neighborhood and our kids went to nice schools. We were not financially rich by any means, but we were doing okay. Our kids played sports, we had bar-b-ques at our house sometimes, and we had plenty of presents under the Christmas tree. My ex-husband had a good job and he was on track to advance. We were a lot more fortunate than a lot of people and we never went hungry.

And then we split up. As if splitting up a family is not stressful enough, I was suddenly the head of the household in my home. My husband moved out and the kids and I stayed in our house for the time being. This house, as with most houses, had a mortgage, utility bills, and other expenses. I needed gas in my car. My kids and I needed to eat. I had no idea where I would get the money. I was terrified. But I also was dealing with everything else that goes along with getting divorced so there were constant distractions. I was consumed with worry about the kids, I was trying to stay afloat in nursing school, and I was trying to, in as civilized a way as possible, work with my ex-husband to sort through splitting up. I was dealing with attorneys, I was dealing with a roller coaster of emotions, and I was trying to put on a brave face for the kids.

Things got worse and I quickly dove to depths of despair that I had not known before. On several occasions, I used gas from the lawn mower fuel can to fill up the gas tank in my car so that I could drive the kids to school. I sometimes rode my bike to the grocery store to get food so that I didn't have to use gas in my car. Numerous times I looked for change in the sofa cushions to see if I could get my kids a treat of Chick-fil-A after school. The water got turned off several times at our house. One year, we went an entire winter with no heat because the central AC/heat was broken and I didn't have the money to fix it. Thank goodness we live in Louisiana and not Minnesota.

Now, I am thinking you are wondering where my family and friends were and why didn't anyone help us out? Well, the short answer is nobody knew. I was so ashamed of our situation that I didn't tell anyone how bad things were. I was too embarrassed. We were a nice middle-class family, with kids in private school, and I just was so ashamed. I didn't tell a single person. I did wind up telling my dad that I could not afford a divorce attorney and he lent me five thousand dollars to pay for that. But other than that, I was too ashamed to tell anyone the whole truth. And I also didn't want to burden anyone else with my problems. I hated to make anyone worried about me. I was convinced that our situation was temporary and I would get it figured out so I didn't see the use in alarming anyone else. Plus, the truth is I was mortified.

I don't know if you have ever been to the depths of financial hell, but it sucks. Nothing feels worse than standing in line at the grocery store with your kids and praying to God that your debit card is not declined. These situations can really make you desperate and it can make your thinking clouded. It can make you feel isolated and hopeless. It can cause you to make some really bad financial decisions. When you don't know where your next meal is coming from, you are not too concerned with your long-term return on investment. One way that I was able to bring in some money was by taking out the maximum amount possible of student loans for nursing school. Not the best idea. But it did give me a couple thousand dollars every semester and, at the time, I did not even remotely care how it would ever get paid back. Other than the student loans, I really don't know how I stayed afloat.

After some time, my ex-husband started giving me monthly child support, which was huge to me. I also graduated from nursing school about a year and a half after we split and started making my own income. Thank God. When I started nursing school, I had no idea I would ever be getting divorced. It had just been a lifelong dream for me to become a nurse and was, honestly, almost more like a hobby. Before divorcing, I really did not need to work. After divorcing, my "hobby" became vital to my survival. I kept thinking to myself God must have known that I would need to support myself one day and that's why he sent me to nursing school.

The years following were exhaustingly rocky financially. My ex-husband was awarded our house in the divorce because there was no way that I could afford to keep it. In the summer of 2015, my kids and I moved out of the house that we had lived in for the past nine years and moved in with my dad. Needless to say, this was humbling. I was a 43-year-old mom with two kids moving back in with Dad. Now, I know people probably do this all the time, but that didn't make it any easier. This only propelled my self esteem further into the ground.

Our move into my dad's house was only meant to be for the summer. The kids and I were going to stay until I could save a little money and then we would move to a new home. My dad was happy to have us and he helped with watching the kids while I worked. So my kids and I spent the summer at my dad's with literally just our clothes in some suitcases. All of the rest of our belongings were in a storage unit.

At the end of that summer, God was looking out for us again. My brother and his wife and kids had just moved. He still owned his old house and he offered to rent it, very cheaply, to me. It worked out perfectly. So we moved again. The kids and I moved all of our stuff out of storage and into my brother's old house. It felt somewhat like we had a little place of our own. I still struggled with making ends meet and money continued to be tight, to say the least, but at least we had a home. We stayed in that cute little house for three years.

What I have learned is that it is so hard for me to admit when things are not okay. And it is so hard to say you are broke. When you are in an upper or middle class environment and you are broke, your lack feels magnified. I would be driving up to a carpool line filled with Range Rovers after I had just filled up my gas tank with lawn mower gas. And, to say the least, that feels pretty discouraging. Although, I truly believe that having no gas money universally feels awful, no matter your demographic.

This whole being broke thing made me feel horrible and like there was truly something wrong with me. Why had I so horribly failed? What had I done to deserve this? Why was I not normal like all the other moms? I was so scared to tell others about my situation because I felt sure they would judge me. And one thing I have found is that, when you're feeling at your lowest and your self esteem has plummeted, you are less likely to reach out and tell others because you feel so awful about yourself. You fear that others may feel the same way about you that you feel about yourself. And that would feel heartbreaking.

I also hate to worry other people. I hate to ask for help. And I don't want to put any extra burden on people who already have a lot on their plate. And I really did believe that, given some time, I would come up with a solution so there really was no need to alert everyone. Ugh.

I was angry, sad, and defeated much of the time. I tried so hard to remain positive though. And I never let my kids see how discouraged I was. I often reminded myself that, compared to some people in the world, I had it made. I tried to remember that I was still blessed and that things could always be worse. At least we were healthy. At least we had a roof over our heads. At least we had food.

And I also tried to remind myself that I may not have been as alone as I felt. If I could be having financial problems, maybe others were also and they were just hiding it like me. Maybe Bobbie Jo driving the Mercedes doesn't know how she will pay her light bill this month either. Maybe Tommy with the Rolex is $850,000 in debt and facing bankruptcy. You never know. Maybe Karen who also looks so perky and happy at the PTA meeting is also secretly going through a crisis of her own. Of course, it wasn't that I wanted this for anyone else. But it made me feel a little less alone if I told myself that maybe there were others struggling like me. And, just for the record, there is absolutely nothing wrong with having Range Rovers or Rolexes. If you can afford it, and it's your heart's desire, go for it! If you have worked hard for it and that's your prize then, honestly, I think that's awesome.

Time went by and I kind of turned into a recluse. I worked, did things with the kids, ate, and slept. I started turning down offers to do things with friends. Either I couldn't afford it or I just didn't want to go. I was exhausted most of the time. And, to make things worse, I also gained thirty pounds during this time. Since I was working so much, I had no time for exercise anymore. I was super stressed. Food was comforting to me. And I was constantly worried about money. I worked sometimes four jobs at a time. I changed jobs multiple times in an effort to find the perfect job that would provide a good salary, give me flexibility to be there for the kids, and be somewhat enjoyable. On more than one occasion I collapsed on the floor of my bathroom, in private, crying because I was exhausted and had no idea how things would ever work out. Multiple times I felt like Will Smith on the subway bathroom floor clutching his kid in *The Pursuit of Happiness*. I don't think it gets a whole lot worse than that. So, I would remind myself that at least I wasn't homeless. At least my kids and I weren't sleeping in a dirty subway bathroom. Nevertheless, there were so many days when I was not sure I could keep going if something didn't change.

This whole time period seems like a blur to me. I was living paycheck to paycheck and constantly trying to figure out how to move ahead. I went through a time of taking out loans to pay off debt only to heavily regret that later. I became so discouraged sometimes that I would say, "Screw it, let's go out to eat," and then I would fall into a pit of regret for having splurged.

During this time, I also started getting discouraged about life in general. I was feeling hopeless about ever making enough money to do the things I wanted. I was feeling depressed at the thought of having to spend the rest of my life working three or four jobs to survive, much less have a nice retirement. I was feeling sad about being alone in my struggle. All in all, I was feeling really sorry for myself. I was definitely stuck in a woe-is-me cycle. Something had to change.

After three years in my brother's house, my ex-husband agreed to grant our house back to me. I had been working for a good while then and had reached a point where I was pretty confident that I could afford the monthly mortgage payments. It would be really tight, but if I was careful with my spending, it could work. The house had been empty and on the market for some time but had not sold, so he decided that he would officially put the house back in my name. For the first time in so long, I thought things were headed in the right direction. Something had gone my way finally. I was certain that this was an indicator of a shift in the right direction and things would start looking up. I had always loved that house so much, so I was super excited.

So, after three years in my brother's house, the kids and I moved again. Three moves in three years. It felt surreal. But I was so glad to be back in my house. I felt like this would be the perfect time to settle in and rebuild my life. I was sure I could now afford the mortgage payments and everything would work out.

Things are finally going my way, I thought. I was absolutely certain that this was the beginning of a big turnaround. My big comeback!

As usual, things didn't go as planned. Isn't there some saying that if you want to make God laugh, tell him your plans? Of course. The first few months back in the house were like a dream. We were so excited to be back "home" and there were suddenly so many things to do like rearranging furniture and unpacking; definitely no time for sitting around and eating donuts or mulling over all of my problems. This whole move really lifted my spirits and jolted me back to feeling like my old self. There was a definite boost to my self-esteem. I was a homeowner! All by myself! I started feeling like I was solidly on track to get my life back together. I would lose the weight, work on being my best self, start socializing more, and turn this life of mine around. Amen!

Unfortunately, there were other plans ahead for me. Around this time, a friend of mine and I had the idea to try to start a new business. We wanted to break away from traditional nursing and build a small business that we really believed in. So I started putting money into that.

I was so excited about it. Things were really coming together now! I became obsessed with the idea of being an entrepreneur and poured a ton of energy into it. When we both weren't working, my friend and I spent hours planning and researching. It was really, really fun and something I never imagined I would do. I kept envisioning myself as a business owner and I pictured myself making my own hours, making more money, and being able to live life on my own terms.

Well, after about six months of giving it a really good try, it didn't go as planned and it never really took off. This was definitely not the end of the world, but I was pretty disappointed. We didn't lose much money, thank goodness, but I felt defeated and sad. For the first time in a long time, I had felt excited about something again. I would wake up in the morning and look forward to my day instead of dreading getting out of bed and having to go to the same old job again. I was starting to see the possibility of a future in which I didn't have to spend the rest of my life working three or four nursing jobs until I died. So having to give up on our business idea was a big letdown.

During this time, I was also in the process of attempting to modify the mortgage on my house. After moving back in, I was actively working with the mortgage company to rectify a past due situation and they assured me that it was not a problem. They told me repeatedly that if I supplied them with the needed paperwork, kept in touch, and tried catching up on payments, everything would work out just fine, no worries. They assured me that they were working to modify my mortgage payment and that, once approved, any past due amount would be built into the modified loan. Perfect.

This whole mortgage modification process went on for at least six months. Meanwhile, I was engrossed in taking care of my kids, working full time, and trying to start a new business. Every once in a while I would get a phone call from the mortgage company and they would need some documents filled out and emailed and I would get that taken care of right away and go on with my life. I wasn't concerned at all by any of this because the mortgage company kept assuring me that all was fine and dandy and that they were working hard to modify my mortgage and make my payment lower. Awesome! And, even better, they assured me that during the mortgage modification process I didn't have to make my monthly mortgage payments if I didn't want to or wasn't able to. Essentially, they told me that I was protected from foreclosure while going through the modification process. They assured me that any missed payments and past due amount would be factored back into the newly worked loan amount that I would start paying on after the process was over. This all sounded promising and like it was perfectly in line with my new, refreshing life that I was building.

Well, as the saying goes, if it sounds too good to be true, it probably is.

I will never, for the life of me, forget this moment. It was a regular Tuesday. The kids were at school. I was working, driving around seeing patients. I was in my car in between patients' houses and my phone rang and I saw it was the mortgage company. I pulled over and answered. I was sitting in my car in a bank parking lot and I heard the person on the other end of the line tell me that my mortgage loan modification application had been denied and I owed $17,000, which had to be paid within fourteen days or my house would go into foreclosure. What? No, seriously, what did you just say? WHAT? Holy fuck. You have got to be kidding me.

I started shaking and crying. I felt like I couldn't breathe. I was so confused and shocked. I thought I might throw up and I opened my car door in case I did. The man on the phone explained that, since my application was denied, $11,000 in late payments and fees and $6,000 in something else that I didn't understand was now immediately due. Fourteen days. Seventeen thousand dollars. I hung up the phone and sobbed like I don't ever remember sobbing before.

Let me just stop here and ask. Have you ever experienced a moment when you feel like the entire world has stopped? Where you feel almost disconnected from the earth? Where you are in complete shock and, honestly, you are not sure if you are alive or dead? Where the world literally stops spinning and you feel as though you may pass out? Where your whole body goes numb and you cannot feel anything? Where you literally have to hold on to something sturdy nearby because you are so dizzy? Well, this was how I felt in this moment. I have only felt this way a few times in my life and most of those times involved finding out that a loved one had passed away or something equally horrifying.

Anyway, I could not see how this could have happened. I was confused and, at first, convinced that the man on the phone had made a terrible mistake. But he hadn't. I called the mortgage company multiple times over the next few days to try to figure out how this even happened. They assured me over and over again that everything was correct and I did indeed owe $17,000 to avoid foreclosure. I did not see a way out of this. I was 100% sure there was absolutely no surviving this mess. I mean how on earth was I going to come up with $17,000 in fourteen days? No really, how? At this point in time I was definitely doing a tiny bit better than just scraping by but I definitely also did not have $17,000 lying around. My balance in my savings account was, on a good day, maybe $250. So I was a solid $16,750 short.

And I had no partner to help me. No spouse to share this pain with. Nobody to help me figure out how to fix this. Nobody to stress with. Nobody to watch the kids while I had a nervous breakdown. And I just couldn't tell my kids about this. I kept it a secret from them. I did talk to my ex-husband several times and he was helpful in doing what he could to help me deal with the mortgage company and understand what was going on. But I was just too ashamed to tell anyone else. I had to figure this one out on my own. Or I thought I did.

There was one thing I was absolutely certain of. I could not lose my house. There was no way, no chance in hell that I was giving this house up. Not after everything the kids had already been through. Not after three moves already. No way. Over the next several days, I repeatedly called the mortgage company and tried to work it out. They offered no help except the option of a short sale. My mortgage company suggested that I call a credit counseling company. So, desperate for any help I could get, I called the credit counseling company and the lady I spoke to told me, "Oh honey, you won't lose your house! You can just file bankruptcy!" Say what? Wait, what? Bankruptcy? That's my only option? I can't file bankruptcy! Bankruptcy is for other people, not me! Bankruptcy is for people on television! Bankruptcy would not be something that I would survive. I was positive about that. In all of my worst-case-scenario nightmares, I had not even considered bankruptcy. Jeez.

After frantically thinking this over for a few days, I decided that I had to do anything I could to keep the house and I had to be open to all options. So, I made an appointment and went to a bankruptcy attorney for a free consultation. This, I would definitely consider to be one of the lowest moments of my life. Just making the phone call and setting up the appointment with the attorney felt soul crushing. But I had to do it.

Anyway, I made the appointment and, using every muscle fiber in my body, forced myself to go. I got dressed, said a few prayers, and drove to the attorney's office. As to be expected, the bankruptcy attorney's office was on one of the busiest streets in our small town. I mean, of course. Had they really not considered this when scouting out locations? Did they not consider that just maybe people would not necessarily want it advertised all over town that their financial life was a disaster? I wanted to put a bag over my head to walk to and from my car and I tried my best to find the most inconspicuous parking spot around.

Nevertheless, I parked my car and made the walk of shame inside. There was a receptionist right in front and she asked me to have a seat on this little couch and wait my turn.

The shame I felt sitting there was absolutely crushing. I felt like an absolute failure.

The bankruptcy attorney turned out to be a really nice lady and she made me feel better about everything. She assured me that I could file for bankruptcy and keep my house. She explained to me the entire bankruptcy process and made it sound like people did it all the time. So, as crazy as this sounds, it actually did make me feel a little better knowing that that was an option if I really wanted to do that. I felt slightly relieved and comforted knowing that I would not have to lose my house if I really didn't want to.

It was around this time that I began to experience a level of anxiety that I had never known. Shocking, right? I was so low. I could not sleep well. I had nightmares. I felt angry. I felt terrified and I felt helpless. I was losing hope. I started being forgetful. I started being constantly on edge. I was snappy and probably looked a bit like a deer caught in the headlights.

I don't know if any of you have ever been faced with foreclosure, but I would bet that in Hell you get foreclosure notices and phone calls every day. I would bet that the dictionary has foreclosure listed as a synonym for torture.

It is absolutely HORRIBLE. And it sucks every ounce of pride and hope and self-esteem right out of you. It makes you feel isolated and terrified in a way unlike any other. You live day to day not knowing if your home will be taken away. You start collapsing in shame worried that people you know will find out about it. You lie awake at night fearing what your kids may go through and how you will explain this to them. Your whole existence becomes fear. You become desperate. And you feel so different than other people. I became 100% convinced that I was the only human on Earth living this way and that, without a doubt, every other human had their shit together and was financially stable. I felt like I was living a lie. A double life. I was consumed with terror about being foreclosed on, and yet I would go out into public and smile and act like nothing was wrong.

For the first time in my life, I wanted to go to work. I wanted to be distracted from the nightmare I was living at home. Once I got home from work, it was back to trying to figure out how to prevent homelessness. Ugh. And I believe this is another reason that I didn't tell any of my friends or family what was going on.

When I was with them, I just didn't want to talk about it. I wanted a little bit of time to be free from the nightmare I was living. I wanted to get lost in enjoying my time with them and forget all my troubles.

Did I also mention that during this entire foreclosure debacle I had no car? You know how when it rains it pours? This was like a monsoon. In the middle of trying to save my house, my car broke down. Twice. The first time I fixed it and the second time it was dead forever. Yes, I fixed it myself at one point (that's seriously a whole other chapter....).

Anyway, the complete desperation I felt at this time was horrifying. Thank God for my brother. He let me borrow his old, really old, pickup truck that he didn't drive. So I spent a solid month, at least, driving around in this old truck with a manual transmission. But, really, who even cares when it's your only option for transportation? But with my already dwindling self-esteem this really made me feel low. I drove the truck for about a month and then I worked out a deal and was able to get a good deal on a long-term rental car. I didn't have the money for a down payment on a car and I definitely didn't have the money to outright buy a car. And I didn't have the guts to apply for financing on a car because how on earth would I explain that I was in the middle of facing a possible foreclosure but could you please lend me twenty grand? Sheesh.

In the end, as things usually do, everything worked itself out. My house technically went into foreclosure, but within a few months I was able to get the money to pay off the past due amount and bring the loan current. Thank the good Lord that the foreclosure process actually takes quite a long time so, even when it starts, you don't have to move out the very next day. I was not aware of this at first so when I found this out, it felt like winning the lottery. And after some time and after driving a rental car for about six months, I was also able to purchase a car of my own.

Maybe it's just me. Maybe other people have their financial lives together and never have to worry. Maybe people make smarter financial choices than me. And maybe people will read this and think, *What on earth is wrong with this girl?* I don't know. Actually, I would imagine that most people really do have their crap together regarding finances. I would imagine that other people maybe do have their shit straight. I really don't even know.

What I do know for sure is this. Money problems are debilitating. Money problems are soul crushing. And for a single parent, on one income, trying to support kids and make a decent life, it can be stressful like nothing else. Trying to provide your kids with the same things their friends have and prevent them from seeming different or less than is so hard. Not to mention the feeling of being less than when your children's other parent has a salary that is five or six times your own. You may be struggling to pay for gas when your child comes home from their house with a brand new Xbox. That hurts. How do you explain to your child that you love them just as much even though you didn't get them everything on their Christmas list like Daddy or Mommy did?

Anyway, I have actually spent time daydreaming about how wonderful it would be to live on a farm in the middle of nowhere, or an igloo in Iceland, or in a hut on a remote island in the Pacific. I daydream about this because I imagine that in any one of these scenarios there would be less financial burden, less financial competition, less need for things. I daydream about a simple life where there is no need to accumulate things, no need to try to impress anyone. I would spend my days working in the garden, baking pies (well, probably burning pies), going for long walks, and reading. I would give all of my money away to charity and keep just enough to eat. I wouldn't give a crap about what other people thought about me. Sounds like bliss to me.

But, in the meantime, I am taking note of the things I have learned (the hard way) along the way:

1. This one is a real shocker but here goes: even if I don't buy my kids every single thing they ever wanted, they STILL love me! No, really! They really do! Believe me, I have loads of experience with this one and it has proven to be true time and time again. And even if I can't measure up financially to my kids' dad, they love me just the same. And quite frankly, if I spend too much money on my kids, they can probably sense that I overextended myself and they may wind up actually feeling bad about it. So

financial boundaries really do make everyone feel better.

2. I can be a scrappy hustler when needed. Not sure if I am super proud of this or not, but it's true. When desperate times come knocking, I can put up a fight. I can sell things on eBay. I can pick up extra shifts at work. I can use lawn mower gas to fill up my car. I can be my own car mechanic. I can come up with $17,000 if I have to. Whatever I need to do to get the job done, I can do it. One thing is for sure, I will go down swinging.

3. Payday loans are a VERY bad idea.

4. Taking out a loan and thinking to yourself, *I will figure out how to pay this back later,* never ends well. I know exactly how it goes. In moments of desperation, it is beyond easy not to give two thoughts to the future. Your only concern is the here and now and surviving this week. And, honestly, you

really do believe that if you take out this loan and then buckle down on saving, you will pay the loan back and it will all work out just fine. Yea, it doesn't really work like that. It really is best to have a solid payback plan before borrowing any money.

5. And last but definitely not least, my personal favorite: the amount of money I have does not equate to my value as a person. BAM! This one took FOREVER to sink in for me. For a very long time I believed that my ex-husband was a better person than me because he had more money than me. I believed that the other parents in carpool line were better than me because they had nicer things. I thought that, because I didn't have my financial life in order, I was a bad person. I thought that because I was broke, I was worthless. Not anymore. I now understand that my net worth has nothing to do with who I am as a person. I understand that my financial status has nothing to do with how kind I am. I realize that the size of my bank account does not determine if I am a good mom. I came to understand that the

kind of car I drive has nothing to do with my value as a human. I realized this by applying my own thinking to other people. If my son was broke, would I consider him a bad person? No! If my friend and her husband lost their house to foreclosure, would I think her value as a human decreased? Definitely not! If my daughter lost her job and all her money, would I see her as less than perfect? No way!

I am no way near being in financial bliss yet, but here is what I know. I know that any financial problems I may have do not define who I am as a person. My bank account is not indicative of my love for my children. And regardless of how much money I have in my bank account, I am still richer than so many others. I have healthy children. I have a roof over my head. I ate three meals yesterday. My heart is bursting with love for my family. I have a super cozy bed. And I am breathing. I am so freaking blessed.

Chapter 9: *Jill of All Trades*

F un fact: I have changed the ignition coils in my SUV. "What's that?" you ask. "What are ignition coils? What do they do?" I have literally no clue.

One of the many fabulous parts of being a single parent is that you are the head of the household. The captain of the ship. The ringleader of the circus. Whether you are a man or a woman, you are the person in charge, which means that everything that needs to be fixed, repaired, built, put away, worked on, taken care of, etc. is your responsibility.

At one point my car started making a funny noise, kind of like a screaming noise. Not only did this embarrass my daughter to her core when I pulled into carpool line, but it also meant that something was probably not right in the engine. Since I am a home health nurse, my car is vital to my job. I have to have an operating car. So I took my car to the shop and, at the end of the day, the mechanic called me and said that my car was shot. He said that, since there was so much wrong with it, it was basically totaled. Seriously? Please tell me you are kidding. When you are a single mom trying as it is to make ends meet, having a "totaled" car is absolutely not an option.

I immediately went to my computer and pulled up a chair. I started googling "my car is screaming." I know, probably not the smartest idea. First, I should mention that I have never in my life had any kind of experience fixing cars and I have never had any mechanic training. I have done small things here and there, like putting air in the tires and changing burned out lightbulbs, but definitely no mechanic work. I have never even understood how car engines work, and when I pop the hood and look underneath, I am completely lost.

After some time on the internet, I diagnosed my car as needing a new PCV valve. Yep, I am not even kidding. I spent hours googling, watching YouTube videos, and reading articles to make this diagnosis. All while having never done a single thing like this before.

So, I started shopping around online and ordered the required part off an auto supply website. And I should mention that money was already super tight. So, I was really taking a massive gamble by ordering some expensive car part off the internet, which, considering my lack of mechanic experience, was probably not going to fix my car. But I kept telling myself that if I could order this part off the internet for two hundred bucks and fix it myself, I would be saving thousands of dollars potentially. And the truth is, since I was pretty much broke at the time, I really didn't have any other options. I could not afford to buy a new car. And I definitely did not have a few thousand dollars lying around to pay for a new engine.

So anyway, this new part comes in the mail about a week later. I wait until my kids are gone to their dad's house for the weekend, and I spend a whole Saturday watching YouTube videos and learning how to replace a PCV valve. Once I felt certain that kind of understood what to do, I headed outside.

I gathered all my supplies and set up my little mechanic shop in the driveway. And, let me tell you, I exert a GREAT deal of effort to make sure that the neighbors (or any other humans) do not see me working on my car.

Let me just stop right here and explain this. For some reason, I always felt shame when it came to things like this. Like if the neighbors saw me working on my car, covered in grease and dripping sweat, they would know what a failure at life I was. They would know that I was broke and couldn't afford to pay a repair shop.

They would know that I was completely alone and had to do things like repair my car all by myself. They would know that I had failed at marriage, was a horrible mom, was terrible at managing money, and I was a terrible person. Well, that's a bit of an exaggeration, but that's honestly how my mind works. And the shame spiral that my mind can sometimes fall into is no joke. In reality, I felt embarrassed to be outside working on my car on a beautiful Saturday afternoon when the other moms in my neighborhood were probably making cookies with their kids or getting their outfit planned for their weekly date night with their husband. I just felt so different. Like from another planet kind of different.

Anyway, as it turned out, my Saturday spent in the driveway getting covered in grease was a success. After a few hours with the hood propped up, my hands and T-shirt and jeans covered in grease, and my phone battery almost dead from watching multiple YouTube instructional videos, I had the new part installed. I took a good look around to make sure no neighbors were watching and I got behind the wheel. I said about fifty silent prayers before I even attempted to try to start it. I was so nervous! With my greasy hand shaking nervously, I put the key in and turned it over. I almost couldn't believe it myself but it started on the first try! I felt like I must have been mistaken when I heard the engine rev up. I mean, did I really just fix my car?! I almost screamed out loud with excitement.

So I drove around the block just to be sure and it ran like a charm. I was so proud of myself! As crazy as it sounds, I felt unstoppable and like I could solve any problem. I rode this high for at least a week. I was telling anyone and everyone that I fixed my car. Need your car repaired? Call me! Need your oil changed? Sure, no problem! Need a new transmission? I'm your girl!

My bubble burst a few months later when I was driving home from the store one night. A few blocks from my house, my car just stopped. It just died. It made some rattling noise for about thirty seconds and then the engine just gave out. I was able to drift it over to the side of the road, thankfully, but I could not get it to restart. After several minutes of panicking and trying to figure out what to do, I got out and walked the rest of the way home.

At this point, I felt like the world had just ended. I can't even begin to describe how devastated and hopeless I felt. It was a regular Tuesday night, my car had just died, and I had to work the next morning. And, like I said before, I drive for my job. I had no idea what to do.

This is one of those times when I longed to be married. I longed for a partner to call who would help me figure out what to do. I longed for someone to make a plan with. I longed for someone to come pick me up and offer to drive me to the car rental place. I longed for someone to tell me everything would be okay.

Instead, I sat alone at home, probably shaking, and tried to figure out what to do. I told myself that, no big deal, I had fixed the car before and I could do it again. I could take the day off work the next day and work on the car. But, seriously, when you are by yourself, there are so many complications in a situation like this. Okay, so I will go to Autozone tomorrow for a car part. Oh wait, how will I get to

Autozone? Okay. So I will rent a car. Oh wait, how will I get to the car rental place? Ugh.

Thank the good Lord, I called my brother and he let me borrow his old truck that he doesn't use. So, I got my son to drive me over to my brother's house and I picked up the truck. No worries that the truck is a stick shift and I am pretty sure it's from like 1987. No biggie. It's a vehicle and it runs! So I went to work and in my free time started googling, once again, how to fix my car. I guess I assumed that by now I was basically a licensed mechanic.

This time I diagnosed the problem as the ignition coils. I determined, after exhaustive internet searching, that I needed to replace them. I know, right? I don't know what I was thinking but, honestly, I was desperate and desperate times call for desperate measures. So I ordered the new ignition coils for around $400. That's $400 that I really could not afford to be spending. The parts came in and, once again, I spent a Saturday afternoon hiding from the neighbors, watching YouTube car repair videos, and working on my car. This time, after hours spent under the hood and with grease caked under my fingernails, my repairs did not work. I followed the instructions exactly as shown, but the new ignition coils did not make my car start up. I tried about 300 times to start the car but it was dead. I had the most awful sinking feeling inside. I just knew that the car was really dead this time. Four hundred dollars and a whole Saturday wasted and nothing to show for it. *What in the mother freaking heck do I do now?* I felt completely defeated and like I might throw up.

Looking back on this whole car experience, I really am not even sure how I got through it without having a nervous breakdown. Really. I was so SCARED the whole time. I literally was operating through life on a minute-to-minute basis. Yes, I definitely learned some new skills. I learned how to make a few repairs on my car. I learned how to use a few tools. I learned how to get grease out of clothing. I learned how to prop up my phone inside the car hood so that I could simultaneously watch an instructional video and look at the actual, real-life, engine. I really did feel like a Jill of all trades. I felt like, given a free Saturday and a good Wi-Fi signal, I could probably tackle any home repair needed.

But, honestly, while going through it, I was not happy to be the Jill of all trades. I really was secretly wishing for a partner to help me out. I really did not want to be the only one responsible for every problem that came up. I wanted a co-pilot.

And there is no way that I can go without mentioning how men must feel when they are in the same situation. I mean, what are they thinking when their 13-year-old daughter says she needs tampons? Or what about when they have to chaperone their son's soccer party and they are the only dad in a room full of moms? Or what about when a dad has never cooked a day in his life and suddenly he has to take over as head chef? Or his daughter needs her prom dress hemmed at the last minute and he has no clue how to use a needle and thread? Or what about when a dad feels equally overwhelmed by the enormity of responsibilities that he has to take on? How does he feel when his car breaks down and he has nobody to pick him up and he has to figure out how to get his kids to school in the morning? I would imagine that he feels equally defeated and desperate.

Anyhow, one thing is for sure. I have learned way more than I ever wanted to on this journey about being independent. In addition to my newfound mechanical skills, here are some other things I have learned along the way:

1. I have become well-rounded. And I am not just talking about my figure. I am talking about all of my new skills that I have had to (well, been forced to) learn. In an effort to have a positive attitude about it, I am trying to focus on how much I now know! Yes, you would be correct in thinking that I have mostly whined and complained when I have had to learn something new like how to fix the garbage disposal. And, yes, I am kind of hoping that I don't have to learn a whole lot more around this house. But why not change my thoughts around and consider myself a badass for learning new skills? Why not pick my head up and feel proud of my capability in managing a household?

2. I am capable of WAY more than I think! Seriously! When my car broke down and I was stranded on the side of the road, I was certain that fixing it was not something I could do. But I did! When I had to get the kids to school and didn't have any gas, I was sure there was NO WAY I could come up with a solution. But I did! And when I saw no possibility of avoiding foreclosure and thought the world was ending, I figured it out! So, according to my track record, there's not much that I can't do!

3. There is no need to feel embarrassed by my head of household position. What I mean is if I feel different because I am trying to repair the lawn mower and that's not something the other moms are doing, it's really okay. I like to try to remind myself that there are people who would give anything to be in my position. There might be a mom who is divorced and wishing she even owned a lawn mower. There may be a dad who is so depressed he can't even get out of bed and he would give anything to

have the energy to cut the grass. There may be kids who have a mom who has to work all the time just to make ends meet and they would give anything to have her home and burning dinner on the barbecue. You really never know.

Looking back on the entire post-divorce time of my life, I can't believe how much I was forced to learn and tackle on my own. Really. I sometimes can't believe I survived. And I don't mean that in a super dramatic, feeling sorry for myself sort of way. I mean it in an "I can't believe I didn't have a big giant breakdown" kind of way. Like I am shocked. The kind of breakdown where you actually have heart palpitations and drive yourself over to the ER because you are sure you are having a heart attack. The kind of breakdown where you declare that you are done. Like really done. With everything. Phew. And let me just say, if you have had one of these types of breakdowns, I feel for you 100% and I totally GET IT. I really, really get it!

Chapter 10: *Dating (check please!)*

I would argue that you do not know what stress is until you're sitting in a fancy restaurant on a date with a guy you just met five minutes ago, having some fancy drinks, and your phone is in your pocket vibrating every 2.2 seconds. When you excuse yourself to go to the bathroom, and you finally get the chance to check your phone, you have about 872 text messages all saying, "Mommy, I miss you," "Mommy, where are you?" "Mommy, please come home." Nothing pulls at your heartstrings more than that. And for me personally, nothing makes my fight-or-flight response kick in stronger. I immediately want to rush home, hug my kids tighter than ever, and tell them that I will never leave them again and then put on my pajamas, get in my comfy bed, and pretend nothing ever happened.

Honestly, I haven't done a whole lot of dating since getting divorced. Well, to be clear, I haven't even been asked on a whole lot of dates or really met anyone single. And I'm pretty sure that one of the requirements of dating is actually getting asked out on a date.

I can't really talk about dating without acknowledging how different dating is when you are forty-something years old, divorced, and have kids. I think the most accurate word to describe it is AWKWARD. First of all, dating again after several decades of being in just one relationship feels like you are going back to high school again or something. Suddenly here you are again worried about your outfit and if you shaved your legs. Making sure you have your Spanx ready to go. Getting nervous about how it will go and what you will talk about. And trying to interpret text messages. And please keep in mind that, when I was in high school, we didn't even have cell phones! Sheesh. And for me personally, literally being concerned about how late this guy will want to stay out. I mean my bedtime now is a LOT earlier than it was when I was in high school. What if he wants to stay out past 8pm?? The horror!!

Anyway, I have been on a few random dates here and there but none of them went remarkably well. One guy, who I had only met about 12 minutes prior (literally), leaned across the table at the coffee shop and told me, "Did you know that the devil wants you to hate Jesus?" Look, it is totally fine and dandy if that is your belief. I can respect that. But I was really thinking the first twelve minutes of a date would, more likely, include talking about things like, "What kind of work do you do?" or "Have you tried the scones here?" Seriously.

I have never tried any dating apps and I just don't think I have it in me to do it. First of all, what would I even put in my bio? Hi there, my name is Summerlin and I am a 46-year-old divorced mom with two teenagers. I would describe myself as exhausted, hungry, and probably on call. I could upload a picture of myself in my worn-out scrubs that I mostly live in. And I could list my hobbies as sleeping, searching Indeed for new jobs, and trying new diets that I won't end up sticking to. Yea, I am not seeing a whole lot of interest in that profile. I know that so many people have had success with dating apps, but I think I'm just going to take my chances and wait for Prince Charming to knock on my front door.

I did date one guy for about a year. It was a pretty rough year. He seemed like a really great guy and I really liked him a lot. But things went downhill quickly. Thanks to him, I now consider myself an expert on red flags. So if you need any advice on red flags and how to identify them, I'm your girl. In an effort to spare you any preventable pain, I am listing here some of the red flags that I have come across while dating as a single parent. Of course there are exceptions to the rule, extenuating circumstances, and out of the ordinary cases, but these red flags are probably pretty general to most situations.

1. Immediately run if the person you're dating
    is still entangled with their former
    spouse/partner/whatever. What's entangled?
    This can mean several things. For instance,
    when your date and his or her ex are having
    sleepovers together, arguing heavily with
    each other, or talking about each other
    constantly. Or, when you walk into your
    date's home and there are photos
    everywhere of their ex, their ex's jacket is
    hanging by the door, and their ex's apron is
    hanging in the kitchen. Or when your date
    is giving their ex free 24/7 access to the
    house with no boundaries. One guy I dated
    for a while often had his ex-wife sleep over
    at the house, her apron still hung in the
    kitchen, photos of her were all over the
    house, she could come and go as she
    pleased, and he talked about her constantly.
    His excuse was that it was all for the kids.
    Hmmm, ok. I mean maybe it was all for the
    kids and maybe that's just what they deemed
    to be the best set-up for everyone involved. I
    don't know. But I can say that it feels off to
    me when you call your boyfriend and he
    doesn't call back and the next morning you
    find out that Mommy had slept over and he

didn't return your call because they were "busy". Call me overly sensitive, but that was a situation that I didn't really want to be in long term.

Before continuing, let me stop right here and take a quick second to explain something. I am 100% in favor of encouraging relationships between parents and their children, and especially after divorce or breakups. As an outsider, I would never want to get in the way of or cause problems with the relationships between children and their parents. I know personally that there need to be boundaries and children's feelings and well-being need to be respected first and foremost. If I am dating a guy, I absolutely do not want to get in the way of his children's relationship with their mother. I want to encourage their relationship and make things easier not more difficult. The point I was trying to make with my first red flag listed above is that if a guy is still very entangled with his ex-wife, he is probably not fully available to you. He probably still has some stuff to work through and, for his and his children's sake, should probably get it all sorted out before bringing another human into the mix. And, honestly, the guy I dated that still had ex-wife sleepover parties is probably a good guy. He just was not in the position to be available for a real, successful relationship at the time.

2. You may want to reconsider if your dream guy/girl is basically using you as a babysitter. Hanging out with your date and his kids for a fun Saturday? Absolutely! I'm in! Going grocery shopping with the whole gang? Sure! Why not? Taking a weekend trip to the beach with all the kids over summer vacation? I can't wait! But on the other hand... Being left with your kids while you go hang out with the guys and I don't know when you're coming back? Not so much. Doing homework with your kids while you are fishing? Ouch. On several occasions I have found myself to be in a situation that felt a whole lot like babysitting. Now, I am not talking about a relationship that has been firmly established and we have relaxed into a normal give and

take routine. What I am talking about is when you are like four dates into the relationship and you find yourself hanging out with the kids instead of your date. I am pretty sure that your gut instinct will let you know when you are, in fact, babysitting and not on a date.

3. You may wish to slow things down if you can't tell if your date is even sober on most occasions. I mean unless, of course, you have a strong desire to be a full-time babysitter while mom or dad sleep off their hangover. Drinks on Friday evening? Fun! Beers at the big game? Of course! Getting high on vacation in Colorado? Why not! But if you regularly smell alcohol, weed, or whatever on your main squeeze at 11:00 a.m. on any given Tuesday, something might be a bit off. Unless you happen to be dating Snoop Dogg. Otherwise, you may be setting yourself up for a lifetime of designated driving and emergency babysitting duties. This might be your cup of tea (or vodka), but it's not for me. Especially when kids are involved, I have never found

it very appealing to be the only adult who isn't blackout drunk.

4. I would suggest to you that you highly reconsider your choice of dinner dates if he cannot keep his eyes on you and off of the 12-year-old looking girl four tables over. Or, if you are a guy, I would reconsider your choice of dance partners if she cannot keep her eyes on you and off the hot 22-year-old dude playing guitar on stage. I went on a date once and I swear I could have been having a seizure and he wouldn't have noticed because his eyes were so fixated on the waitress who I swear could not have been over 15. And considering the fact that, at the time, I had a young teenage daughter, I wanted to vomit. Not only did I feel completely unattractive and miserable sitting there while he ogled another female, I was also completely concerned that I may, in fact, be on a date with a guy who was highly attracted to young teen girls. Yikes. I have also had the misfortune of being on a double date with another couple and I watched, in horror, as the woman in the other couple

actively flirted with and couldn't keep her eyes off of the cute young waiter. I mean shouldn't ALL of the attention from your date be on YOU? And, although it does seem extra creepy to me for a man or woman to be ogling teenagers, the truth is that it doesn't matter what age the object of their attention is. They should only have eyes for you! And don't even get me started on if they are paying more attention to their phone. Unless there is something going on at home with their kids and they need to handle it, for the love of all things holy, they should not be looking at their phone. I once went on a date with a guy and, I am not even kidding, ten minutes into the date he started looking at his phone and responding to texts. I literally sat there awkwardly in silence for a few minutes while he texted. I felt like shit. And I was honestly mortified because at one point the waiter even kind of gave me a pathetic look like he felt sorry for me. Ouch. Somebody told me that I should have taken out my phone and texted him, "Wish you were here." I seriously wish I would have. But, note to self, if your date is more interested in other things in the room besides you, you should probably just ask for the check and call it an evening.

5. Did your date just split up with their wife of 22 years and the mother of his seven children less than five minutes ago? Did your date lose their spouse in a tragic car accident yesterday? Did your date take off their wedding ring as they walked into the restaurant to meet you? Obviously every relationship is different, but, seriously, I don't know how any person can really be ready to date unless they have had at least a little time to themselves. I don't think it is possible for a person to be fully available to you until some time and distance have occurred, especially when kids are involved. He or she may be a great catch, but everybody needs a good minute or two to get themselves together before getting back out there. One of my friends once had a guy send her a message through a dating site and, when asked about his relationship status, he said that his wife of 12 years (12 years!) was killed in a car accident the

month before. I mean has there even been a funeral yet?

I can absolutely say, without a shadow of a doubt, that I was a hot mess right after my ex-husband and I split up. I believed that divorce was the best for us, but I still had mounds of emotions to work through. Honestly, it took me a good few years to even start feeling like myself again. It's been over seven years now and I feel pretty darn good, but it has definitely taken time. And seriously, if you are repeatedly attracting unavailable partners into your life, any therapist would probably argue that you yourself are, at least on some level, unavailable. And I can say with certainty that I spent a solid chunk of my initial post-divorce time being unavailable.

I could probably think of more red flags but these were the ones that came to my mind first. The thing is that dating when you are a single parent is just so different. It's not just about you anymore. So many things to consider besides just picking which movie you are going to see. When should I introduce him to the kids? Should I tell the kids he is just a friend? How does he treat his own kids? Are we going to be like the Brady Bunch? What if he yells at my kids? What if he is amazing and everything I could ever ask for?

I think there should be a dating app for single parents that cuts straight to the point because, in reality, I would argue that single parents are pretty strapped for time as it is. Like I would like to know if you would mind if I am sound asleep at 8:30 p.m. on any given night because I am so freaking exhausted. I would like to know if you mind if we do lots of stuff with the kids because that's really what makes me happy. Do you like going to Disneyworld? What are your thoughts on vaccinations? Also, I would really like to know if you are okay with camping because that's a big thing in my family and I kind of don't want to give it up.

Also, it would be really hard to talk about dating as a single parent and not mention how it can be such a blow to your self-esteem when your ex is already in another relationship and moving things along and you are still full-blown single. I struggled with this for quite some time. I kept thinking that something must be really wrong with me since he could so easily skirt into a brand-new relationship and I had nothing more than a list of dates gone wrong under my belt. What was wrong with me? And every time I went on a date (which was honestly only a handful of times) and it didn't work out, I only felt more convinced that I was a failure and would certainly never be in a relationship again. Every date gone wrong was a gentle reminder to me that my ex was successful and moving on and I was doomed to be single and unwanted forever. Ugh. It's hard not to get a little jealous and it's also hard not to feel deflated and defeated when this happens.

       I don't know if I will ever get married again. I mean I am definitely not against it. But I also definitely don't really have a giant urge to get divorced again either. No thanks. And, yes, throughout this whole book I have mentioned multiple times how horrible it is to feel so lonely. But when considering some of the dating disasters I mentioned in this chapter, I should make it clear that I am not THAT lonely. Like not lonely enough to spend my time with a guy who is blackout drunk most days of the week. Or not lonely enough to date a guy who spends fifty minutes out of every hour talking about his ex. Hopefully, a nice guy who's funny and likes my kids will come along one day and we can ride off into the sunset. Until then, I get to keep the whole king-sized bed to myself. And I am just fine with that.

Chapter 11: *Rock Bottom*

I don't use drugs. I don't really ever drink. I don't make questionable investments that may land me in jail. I am not in the mob and I don't smuggle cocaine across the border to Mexico. I don't engage in any acts that might prompt a large man dressed in all black to come to my house at 2:00 a.m. and put my and my children's feet in cement and dump us in the river.

I never overdosed on heroin and I never went on a drinking bender that lasted eight days and culminated in me waking up naked in a gutter. I never got hauled off to jail because of something illegal I had done. I never collapsed to the floor in defeat and couldn't get back up. There was never a particular moment for me when I said to myself, "Yep, this is it, I have hit rock bottom." There was no exciting, dramatic climax where I hit rock bottom and then everything changed in an instant.

But let me tell you, rock bottom is still possible. What does rock bottom look like for me? Rock bottom would amount to waking up one morning, looking in the mirror, and realizing that the person you see is the furthest from where you thought you would ever be. The person in the mirror is thirty pounds overweight. The person in the mirror has no life savings. The person in the mirror is facing possible bankruptcy and possible foreclosure. The person in the mirror feels defeated. The person in the mirror feels full of shame. The person in the mirror is tired of the struggle and feels so gosh darn far from who I always thought I would be. I would say that, for me, rock bottom was more of a season in my life instead of a single point in time. But when I was going through it, I did 100% recognize that I was at my own personal rock bottom.

My whole life I have been known to be a happy person, always smiling and laughing. And really, at my core, that is how I am. I like to think that I am a positive thinker, a glass-half-full kind of person, a find the humor in the mess kind of person. And DEFINITELY a laugh at a funeral kind of person. But look, there is only so much laughing you can do when it comes to bankruptcy. There is only so much smiling allowed when discussing foreclosure. There are only so many jokes you can make about the electricity being cut off. And things aren't quite so funny when you are trying on bathing suits with an extra thirty pounds on your body.

I definitely was at my own personal rock bottom. There were no dramatic climaxes like I woke up one morning in a gutter or the repo man showed up at my house or I put a bikini on and then ran into Josh Duhamel on the beach. But seriously, this was the bottom for me. How do I know? Because I started praying all the time. I mean ALL the time. Please God, help me to get myself out of this. Please God, help me to change my life. Please God, help me keep going. Please God, show me the way. Please God, don't let me lose hope.

I have always been a praying person. I have always been a spiritual person. And I have always had faith in something greater than me. But this time in my life brought about a whole new level of praying. I would get down at the side of my bed, at least a couple times a day, and pray like I had never prayed before. I would pray in my car while driving. I would pray when I closed my eyes to go to sleep at night. I would pray in the shower. I would ask God to give me the strength to get through another day. I would ask God to watch over my kids. I would ask God to show me the right path and to please, please, please make the correct choices obvious to me. I begged God to light the right paths up to me like a neon-lit billboard. I was so fatigued from making decisions and I no longer had any confidence in my decision-making skills. I was totally spent. I no longer trusted myself to make the right decisions because it seemed to me like I had not made a single right decision in the past, which was why I was even in this hot mess.

I would wake up every single morning and write in my journal. I would make a list of all the things I was grateful for. I would also write out my fears and ask God to take them from me. This may sound super crazy, but I would lastly write out my dreams for the future. And I would write them in the present tense. I had heard people like Wayne Dyer, Louise Hay, Rachel Hollis, and several others all say that this was the way to do it so it MUST be effective. And I was willing to try anything. So my journal read something like this:

Dear God, thank you so much for today.

Thank you for waking me up this morning and giving me another day.

Thank you for my kids.

Thank you for this delicious coffee and this quiet morning.

Thank you for my life.

I am so scared and I feel hopeless, please
help me move through this.

I feel terrified of making the wrong choices.

I feel so scared of losing my house.

I feel so scared of having no money and not
knowing what to do.

Please, dear God, show me the way.

Please give me the courage and faith to keep
going.

Please walk me through this and send me
signs to know you are with me.

Please watch over my kids.

Thank you so much.

And then....

1. I have a job that I love so much! And I
   get paid soooo much money!

2. I have no debt!

3. I am able to give back so much money and help others. It feels so good!

4. I have a beautiful home at the beach!

5. My kids and I are healthy, happy, and thriving!

6. I get to travel often and money is no expense!

7. I am in love with my life!

Crazy? Maybe so. But it got me through the darkest times. There were so many times over the last 10 years when I just had no faith. I was sure that I was being punished for something and that God had forgotten about me. I would drive in my car and think to myself, *Is this really my life? Is this really where I have ended up? How did this happen? And, if this is*

*how the rest of my life is going to go, I am
honestly not even sure I want to keep going.*

I felt so detached from the reality around
me. I felt so different from everyone else. I felt
like I was living a life that nobody else I knew
would ever comprehend. Everyone else I knew
had a seemingly "normal" life. At the age of 45
or so, the people I knew, my friends, other local
parents, were living a life that SEEMINGLY
was the complete opposite of mine. Other
people my age were planning their next
vacations, posting on Facebook about their 20th
wedding anniversary, busy trying to plan their
daughter's sweet sixteen extravaganza, posting
on Instagram about their Christmas shopping
trip to New York, worrying over which book
would be the best to read at the beach. I wanted
so badly for that to be my life. I just wanted to
be "normal". *How on earth could anyone even
relate to me?* I thought. And there was no
possible way that I could even remotely be
honest about my actual circumstances in casual
conversation. Like, "Hey you! What are you up
to this weekend?"

"Oh, you know, not much, I just need to
gather documents and print out tax returns for
the bankruptcy attorney and then I will probably

work on fixing part of my fence that's broken and then I will probably eat a bunch of cookies and pass out in a carb coma. You?"

Or maybe something like, "How have you been?"

"Oh, well, I have been the usual. You know, mainly depressed, anxious, and losing hope. But other than that, fantastic!"

All of these feelings and realities made ME uncomfortable. There was no possible way that I was going to subject anyone else to the discomfort. But, more than ever, I felt like a failure and a misfit.

And can I stop right here and mention how I feel like social media can be soul crushing? Nothing makes you feel more inferior than looking at pictures of everyone else's "perfect" life when you are barely hanging on. Nothing makes you feel like more of a failure when you are so dramatically at the other end of the spectrum than your friends you see on Facebook. And I am 100% guilty myself. I have participated. I have posted pictures of myself and my kids on vacations. Vacations that I may or may not have been able to comfortably afford. And I have, many times, after putting a picture of us on Instagram, felt sad afterwards.

Like I was part of the problem. And the sad truth is, if you take a good look at my Instagram or Facebook posts from over the years, you won't see any signs of loneliness, pain, or financial distress. You will only see the filtered version of my life.

This whole rock-bottom season came on like a train. I remember exactly when it started. Things actually seemed to be going good at the time. No major problems. Obviously, for several years, things had been quite up and down, but nothing compared to this whole rock-bottom thing. It all started when my car broke down.

It was after Christmas, around the end of the year, and my car gave out. I talked earlier about my adventures in mechanics and trying to fix my car, but I didn't really get into how this was the start of a seriously horrible time for me. It all started when I didn't have a car. The stress was starting to build and major anxiety was creeping in. While I figured out what on earth to do with my car I had to rent one.

I rented this little car from Enterprise and drove it for a couple of weeks. The problem was that I still owed money on my broken down car. I was not eligible for another car loan because I still owed money on my current car and my credit was not fabulous. I did not have the money to buy a car outright. So I had to rent a car, which sucked because I would be paying for the rental car plus my monthly car note on my broken-down car.

Well, okay, so I get the rental car. *Okay, I think to myself, I have a car, I can work, and I will figure this all out.* Not so fast. About two weeks into me having the rental car, I backed into a pole with it. I put a large scrape and dent on the back bumper. Oh my God, I thought I was going to die right there. I had not wrecked ANY car since I was a teenager. I had a great driving record, and, considering that I drive every day for my job, that's pretty awesome. But seriously, I drive a rental car for just two weeks and I wreck it! I was so upset. I remember starting to shake a little when it happened and thinking to myself, *What in the hell is going on?* And here's the kicker... I didn't buy the stupid insurance offered by the rental place. It was like thirty dollars a day and I needed the car long term so that would add up to like a gagillion dollars. And I had thought to myself, *What are the odds I will wreck this?* Oh Lord, I should have known.

At the time, I thought to myself, *Okay, this is getting to be more than I can handle.* I kept thinking of that quote, "God will only give you as much as you can handle". Well, I was starting to think to myself, *Um, hello God, so um maybe you got distracted, but, while you weren't looking, I was given way more than I can handle. So if you could just go ahead and turn things around now, that would be fantastic. Thanks.*

A few days went by and, after I got over the initial panic of putting a dent in the rental car, I sucked it up and took it back. I walked into the rental car place feeling like I was going into the principal's office. I had no idea what the rental car companies did in these instances. And, to make matters worse, I still needed a car so I would have to ask them if I could give them back the wrecked car and have another. Oh, for the love. Anyway, thank you baby Jesus, that day I was lucky enough to be served by a young gentleman who was kind and understanding. And he made me feel like it was no big deal. He said it happened often and that my personal insurance should cover it. Phew. I felt like a weight was lifted off my shoulders and I could breathe again. I thought that things were certainly bound to turn around now. I still had no car of my own and I was still paying for both my broken car and the rental car. But I figured that I could work it out in time.

Even though I was still holding out hope that things would get better soon I had started to experience more anxiety. On some level, I had started to think to myself that maybe things could get worse. I started to have a fear in the back of mind about what would go wrong next. I started to feel like I was operating on alert, like anything could happen at any moment. I started to feel anxiety about my car. I didn't know if I should spend the money to get it towed and try to have it fixed or if I should just forget it and try to save for a new car.

A few weeks went by and then I got some good news. I would be eligible, through my job, for a company car in a few months. This was great news but it presented more anxiety. I didn't know if I should wait for the company car, try to get my car fixed, or forget both and buy a new one. You may be thinking that this is an obvious question or that it's not that big of a decision. But when you are suffering from a case of anxiety, this is a bad position to be put in. And I was longing for a spouse/husband/whatever to help me figure it out. I wanted so badly to have someone with me. I wanted someone to talk through the options with. I wanted someone who was also invested in the situation to have an opinion. I did have my brother to talk to about it. My brother is amazing and would probably do literally anything he could to help me. But I didn't tell him everything. First, I was embarrassed. Second, I didn't want to worry him. Third, I didn't want to take up any of his time because he has enough on his plate already. I probably should have told him. Anyway, I decided to keep renting the rental car and wait for a company car.

After a few weeks went by, things were kind of settled. I was still trying to work with the mortgage company to modify my loan; I had the rental car and no more wrecks and no other major crises had arisen.

And then, like I mentioned previously, I got the unanticipated call from the mortgage company that literally felt like a punch in the gut. My mortgage modification had surprisingly been denied and I had two weeks to pay $17,000 or else my house would go into foreclosure. If there was ever a moment in my life that I thought I would not recover from, this was it. I had not seen this coming at all. I was shocked. I felt detached from the world, and I remember thinking to myself, *How can all these people be just going on with their lives like normal when the entire world has just collapsed?*

I spent the next several days desperately calling the mortgage company, googling options, and trying to figure out what to do. I started to wonder if I were living inside a bad dream. I didn't think I lived in a world where I ever would have to file bankruptcy. I didn't think I lived in a world where I thought I would be facing foreclosure. I didn't think I lived in a world where everything went wrong all at once. I didn't ever think I would live in a world where I would feel so alone and so beaten. This is when I knew, without question, that I was at rock bottom.

I kept wondering to myself, *How did I get here? Am I being punished? Will I survive this? How did I get to be a 45-year-old single mom, working four jobs as a nurse, with no car of my own and facing either foreclosure, bankruptcy or both?* Why did everyone else SEEM to have it so easy? Why couldn't I just be normal?

And why did I have to go through this alone? I was longing for a husband to just be beside me through this. It's not that I necessarily needed to be in a relationship at that time, but I kept thinking how much easier it would be if I had someone to talk to who cared as much as I did about all these problems. I kept thinking how, if I had a husband, at least there would be another human being on this earth that understood what I was going through. At least there would be another human who could help me make decisions and help me decide what, if anything, to tell the kids.

What got me through this time? Hours of "Everybody Hurts" by REM on my earphones. How many times have I listened to that song? No less than 871,980,342 times I am sure. What else? Lots of donuts and ice cream. Listening to motivational speeches on YouTube. Watching movies like *I Can Only Imagine* and *The Pursuit of Happiness*. Lots of bubble baths. Lots of cursing. But above all else, my kids.

Every time I would think of my kids, I would try to imagine what I would tell them if they were in the same situation. I hope to God they never are. But what if they were? What advice would I give them? What if my daughter became a single parent and had no income? What if my son was facing bankruptcy?

I would tell them to hold on. I would tell them to keep going. I would tell them to keep praying and not lose hope. I would tell them that it may take some time but things will get better. And I would tell them that, no matter how bad things seem, no matter how unfixable things seem, no matter how hopeless things look, it will be okay. Everything will be okay and you absolutely can survive it. What may look unsurvivable can be survived.

I also frequently used my imagination to remind myself what really matters. I would visualize myself living in a world with no other people besides me and my kids. I would be all alone with just the two of them. And I would think to myself, okay, so of course I want to keep my home and it matters to me if it gets taken away, but living in a world with just my kids, does it really matter if I file bankruptcy? Honestly, in a world with just me and my kids, does this house really even matter? If I lost it, I am sure we would find another place to live. In a world without the opinions of friends, family, neighbors, and others, who really cares about anything except for having each other? Who would really care about anything but the fact that we are healthy, we have food, a warm place to sleep, and each other?

Somebody once told me that anxiety stemmed from the need to please. That anxious feelings arise when we are trying to please others and we are abandoning ourselves. It's the abandoning of ourselves that creates the stress and anxiety. I believe this like nothing else. So, in order to try to free myself from some of the pain and anxiety surrounding my problems, I pretended to be living on a deserted island with just my kids. Nobody else. No other humans to judge us and how we live. Like, seriously, think of Tom Hanks in the movie *Castaway*. Do you think he was concerned at all about what his hair looked like? Do you think he was worried about what brand of volleyball he was sporting? Do you think he felt embarrassed that his homemade loincloth didn't have a Gucci symbol on it? I think not. I would venture to guess that his only concerns were food, comfort, health, surviving, and love—even if the love was for his volleyball. And I am pretty sure he wanted to get off that damn island.

Yes, I totally get that this thinking sounds so weird. But my point is that when you strip away all judgment and trying to impress other people, you are left with what really matters: health, love, comfort, hope, and survival.

So, for a solid few years (and I still do it sometimes), I would drive around in my car pretending like there were no other humans on the planet besides me and my kids. And it helped! When there are no other people, you cease to care what other people think! And truly, what I really wished was that my self-esteem was strong enough that I honestly didn't care what other people thought without having to create some pretend fantasy where there are no other people. I wished that I had a rock-solid foundation of self-worth and self-love and didn't give two flips about other people's opinions. But I didn't. I definitely didn't. I wouldn't say that my self-esteem has ever been crazy high, but when you factor in divorce, serious weight gain, financial collapse, etc., self-esteem is first on the list to go.

But, as with all obstacles and setbacks in life, I learned a lot from my rock-bottom experience:

1. Don't lose hope. Everything can and will work out. It really, really will. I swear. No matter how seriously shitty it gets. Even when you are absolutely, without a doubt, 150% sure that it won't. Even when you are told you have 14 days to come up with $17,000 or else your house will foreclose. Even when you go on eight million dates and none of them work out. Even when you don't know how you will come up with the money to buy your kids Chick-fil-A. Even if the water gets turned off because you didn't pay the bill. Even when your kids leave to go see their dad and you are not sure you will survive the loneliness. I promise that if you keep on trucking and keep on doing the next right thing, it will all work itself out and get better.

2. In the end, all that really matters is each other. All that matters is that we are healthy, have a roof over our heads, have food to eat, and have each other. What's most important are those moments we have spent laughing until our stomachs hurt, singing together in the car on road trips, and just being there

with one another. I wouldn't trade that for all the money in the world.

3. Worrying is such a big freaking waste of time! I repeat, worrying is such a big freaking waste of time!! Can you receive that? Please, please do because I seriously wish I had figured this out a LONG time ago. If I had a dollar for every minute I wasted worrying, well, let's just say I would never have to worry about foreclosure again, on any of my twelve homes...

4. Rock bottom is only a season and it will end. There were so many days over the last few years when I just felt certain that the bad times would not stop coming. I was so low that I was sure I could never recover. And I was convinced that there was something inherently wrong with me and I was being punished. I felt like I was sure I couldn't handle one more bad thing happening and then, BOOM, another bad thing would happen. It felt like I was trying to stay standing in 15 foot waves. But then, little by

little, things turned around. It was slow and took a lot longer than I wanted, but things started looking up. I felt like I was coming out of a dark cave I had been trapped in for years. And, ever since, things have gotten better and better. And now I am so much better and all of the pain and anxiety are gone. And I can honestly say that I am so grateful to have survived that season. And I never want to go through that again!

5. What fear? I am going to present you with a novel idea here. If you go through a rock-bottom phase in your life and you survive, not much scares you anymore! No, really! I have been through near foreclosure and bankruptcy and I worked it out. So, when I consider the idea of that happening again? No big deal. No worries. I'm sure I can work it out. I literally don't feel scared of that anymore and I am now confident that I could figure it out. When I think of being left all alone for a week in the summer while my kids vacation with their dad? Sounds just fine to me. I just might plan my own darn vacation for those days. When I think of my

car possibly breaking down on the side of the road again? Been there, done that. No problem, I'll figure out what to do. And while I walk the two miles home to my house, I think I will put in my earphones and listen to my favorite songs.

If you are a single mama or single daddy and you are at a low point, I am right there with you. I get it. I understand. I have been there and done that and don't want to go back. I hope you find the strength to keep going and I hope you move quickly through rock bottom. It does get better. Just hang in there. Just keep doing one day at a time and know that this season will end. And when your time in rock bottom is over, you will be a member of the survivors' club and you can happily kiss that crap goodbye!

Chapter 12: *The three of us*

T here is a quote by Sigmund Freud that says, "One day, in retrospect, the years of struggle will strike you as the most beautiful." I first came across that quote a few years back, probably around the time when I was marching myself into the bankruptcy attorney's office. Or maybe it was around the time when I was devastated and crying on the floor because it was the first time my kids went to their dad's house for the weekend and I was all alone. Or maybe it was actually around the time when I had no life savings and my car broke down for the second time.

I don't know when it was, but the fact is the first time I heard it I wanted to punch someone in the throat. This was the stupidest and most ignorant quote I had EVER heard. I mean really. How on earth could you look back at near foreclosure and think it's beautiful? How could you look back at constant concern over your kids' post-divorce feelings and think, *Hmmm, what a lovely time*? How could you look back at a scene in which you are filling your car's gas tank with lawn mower fuel and think, *Well, how amazingly beautiful*? This whole "struggle is beautiful" idea was a big load of crap in my opinion. CRAZY!

Well, here we are several years later and I can now say that, yes, it's true, hindsight is 20/20. That whole period of around seven or so years WAS beautiful. I know, right? I must be completely nuts. But I am not kidding here. With every part of my being, I really do look back on that time and see it as beautiful. Why? So many reasons. Let me explain.

During those years, it was just the three of us, me and my two most favorite people taking on the world. And, yes, it was hard. And, yes, without a doubt, I was pretty miserable a lot of that time. But still, there will probably never again in my lifetime be a period where it is just the three of us. My kids are older teenagers now. My son is off to college. My daughter will be off to college soon and, in the meantime, she is pretty much consumed with school and her friends. As crazy as it sounds, I sometimes wish I could turn the clock back and do it all again. I sometimes wish I could take the kids and go back to that little house of my brother's. I might go back and relive the Christmases and barbecues and just being snuggled together in that little house. I know, call me crazy. But really, if I could go back, I might do it all over again. But this time I would try to embrace it a little more. Maybe relax and trust the process a little more. Maybe not worry so freaking much.

So I am going to take this time to reflect on a few things I learned (as usual, the hard way) along the way:

1. Single parenting is NOT for the faint of heart. I mean really. You have to have some serious strength for this gig. And that, in and of itself, is something to feel proud of. And if you don't have the strength to start out with, you darn sure will have acquired it by the time you are done.

2. Even though I will always feel regretful of putting my kids through divorce, I feel so blessed in that I really believe my kids and I have a stronger bond because of it. I believe we have a special kind of relationship that I am not 100% sure we would have had if my ex-husband and I had not gotten divorced. We have been through a lot together and I think we are all a little more grateful for each other. I know I am.

3. Just because our family is different from a lot of the families in our neighborhood doesn't mean that our family is less important or not as special. We might look a little different on the outside from Tommy's family down the street, but we are just as much a family. We eat together, we laugh together, and we love each other just as much as everyone else. And we care about the same things. The important things like love and health and happiness.

4. What is that Charles Dickens quote? "It was the best of times; it was the worst of times." That basically sums up divorcing and becoming a single parent.

5. It is what it is. And that's okay! No, seriously! So many times over the last few years I have been at war with my circumstances. Trying to cover up how bad things really were. Trying to predict and avoid the next disaster. Trying to keep up with the Joneses while I could barely pay for lunch. So much unnecessary internal

turmoil. What if I had just stopped for one second and acknowledged that, okay, this is where I am and I don't have to feel shame for this. This is what's going on and I don't have to pretend it's not. Maybe if I would have made peace with where I was it wouldn't have been such a burden to bear. And maybe I would have felt just slightly less anxious.

6. No matter how bad I think I have it, there will always be somebody who has it WAY worse than me. It's important to really try to comprehend this sometimes. On days when I was really at a low point and doing the whole woe-is-me thing, I thought my problems were just the most horrible thing ever. I was convinced I had been dealt the worst hand. Don't get me wrong, it is definitely important to acknowledge problems and not to diminish feelings about how hard things can get; but, like I have said previously, the problems I have written about in this book, even though they felt GIANT to me, were still minor in comparison to the problems some people

have. Foreclosure? At least I have a house to begin with. There are people in this world who sleep every night on the GROUND. Can't buy my kids Chick-fil-A? There are children on this planet who are actually starving and would give anything for any kind of food. Embarrassed about putting lawn mower gas in my car? There are women alive today who will never, in their entire lifetime, own a car. And, above all else, there are moms and dads and kids on this planet who are sick, or hurt, or dying. There are moms and dads who have lost babies and babies who have lost moms and dads. Now that is HORROR. How could I possibly, even for one second, take for granted all the things that I do have? If foreclosure or bankruptcy or being without a car is the worst hand I'm dealt, then I am one lucky girl.

7. This is my life and I need to get to living it! Last summer, while on a vacation with my kids, I had an epiphany. It occurred to me that the bad times are over and now I need to get to living! It's time for me to pull myself

up by the bootstraps, dust myself off, and get back out in the world. I need to start living again, having fun, doing things that feel good, and just being involved in life again. Yes, I am a divorced single mom, but that is not an excuse to not be living my absolute best freaking life! And, maybe more importantly, I want to teach my kids about life seasons. I want them to know that, even though you may go through a rough patch, things will turn back around. I want to show them, through my own actions, that you can go through hell and survive. You really can pull yourself together, put the bad stuff behind you, and start living your darn life again.

If I already lost you because you don't believe me and think everything I just said is bullshit, let me explain. I totally get it. You may be thinking, *Girl, you don't know what you're talking about. I owe $18,000, my car died FIVE times, and I have been on twice as many bad dates!* I hear you. And, yes, there will most definitely always be somebody who has it way worse than I ever did. But I really do believe everything I said above to be true. Let me give you some examples.

Every time something happened that I was absolutely certain I would not survive, I did survive. When I got the call that I owed $17,000? Survived it. When I shuddered with humiliation as I walked into the bankruptcy attorney's office? Survived it. When my car broke down and I had no means of transportation and didn't know how I would get to work? Survived it. When I put a bathing suit on while thirty pounds overweight and took a swim class at the local gym? Survived it (barely).

Look, I am absolutely not talking here about horrible or tragic things like having a deathly sick child or getting in a horrible car accident. I mean if something terrible happened to one of my kids, I might not survive that. I really might not.

Instead, what I am talking about here are situations that don't actually impact the fundamental well-being of you and your kids. I am talking about situations that still leave you with your health, food, a roof over your head, and each other intact. If these things are threatened, then, yes, I would worry too. But I really, really believe that as long as you have these things, everything else will work itself out.

I recently met a great person who, at the ripe old age of forty something, suffered a stroke. Forty something years old. Partially paralyzed and spends much of the time in a wheelchair now. I cannot even imagine. Just thinking about this really hit me hard. That could be me. That could literally, 100% be me. And when considering this, it becomes crystal clear what really matters. Compared to having a stroke, facing foreclosure is nothing. Compared to being partially paralyzed, whining about gaining thirty pounds sounds so selfish. Compared to spending most of the time in a wheelchair, I will choose walking into the bankruptcy attorney's office any day. In the grand scheme of things, I am, even during the most difficult times, tremendously blessed. Even on my worst days I have so much more than so many other people.

And as far as worrying goes, what a big, fat waste of time and energy. Had I known at the time that everything I mentioned above would work out just fine, I really hope I would have just relaxed and rolled with the punches. I mean that definitely sounds easier said than done. But, really, I blame stress and worry for so many sleepless nights. I blame stress and worry for my thirty-pound weight gain. I blame stress and worry for my massive drop in self-esteem. What a sad thing. On the bright side, I now have a much more solid sense of faith and trust. I believe in my ability to work my way out of problems and I trust the universe to take care of me.

When I look at other people who have not gone through divorce or have not experienced being a single parent or not put lawn mower gas in their car, I see things differently now. I used to feel envious of these people and, honestly, on occasion I still do. I used to think that they were better than me and had their stuff more together than I ever would. I used to think how nice it must feel to never know the sadness of divorce and to never lie awake at night feeling guilty about damaging your kids. But I can now also see the beauty in what I have been through. I can see the strength I have built through surviving. I can see the empathy I have developed for anyone going through the same situation.

When I started writing this, it was mainly just for me. I intended to write it in order to get it all out of me. I was basically writing in my journal. But then I realized that if there was some other mom or dad going through the trenches and feeling all alone, maybe reading this would help them to know that they are, in fact, not alone. Maybe they could escape for a few minutes by laughing at my misfortune.

Above all else, I have learned just how crazy thankful I am for my two kids. Considering everything they have been through, my biggest hope is that they live the rest of their lives filled with happiness and love.

As for me, I would do it all over again just to spend more time with them. And my favorite memories will always and forever be time spent with just the three of us.

Thank you so much for reading!

I hope you have enjoyed reading this as much as I have enjoyed writing it.

It would mean so much to me if you would leave a review for my book! You can return to Amazon or wherever you made the purchase and should be able to easily leave a review. Thank you!

You can always keep in touch with me by following me on Facebook and Instagram

@summerlinconner

You can also find more info and sign up for my newsletter at

www.summerlinconner.com

And, lastly, you can always email me at

summerlin@summerlinconner.com

I would love to hear from you!

Summerlin Conner is an author, Registered Nurse, and mom to two awesome kids. The Three of Us is Summerlin's first book. Summerlin and her kids live outside of New Orleans, Louisiana.

Made in the USA
Columbia, SC
02 March 2021